"Elijah Wreh has a wonderful way of communicating Christ's love for all mankind. It is simple and down-to-earth to read. He will unpackage John 3:16 for you in such a way that you will know that you have been touched by God."

—JERRY KNOBLET, Instructor, John W. Rawlings School of Divinity, Liberty University

"John 3:16 is perhaps the best-known verse in the Bible. It is also the most important. In this well-written, insightful book Dr. Elijah Wreh explains with crystal clarity the meaning and continuing relevance of the message of John 3:16. This is a book you will want to share with family and friends."

—CRAIG A. EVANS, Distinguished Research Professor, The Bible Seminary, Katy, Texas

"In this straightforward book on the most quoted scripture in the Bible, Wreh breaks down John 3:16 for the everyday reader. He takes the familiar terms and concepts found in the passage and provides a theological explanation for each. His intention in this work is simply to proclaim the basic Gospel message that God offers all of humanity salvation, and that salvation is found in Jesus Christ who died for the sins of the world. Although this message is clear but often taken for granted, the author opens up the text in a fresh new way with its challenging questions and devotional context."

—PETER J. BELLINI, Professor of Church Renewal and Evangelization in the Heisel Chair, United Theological Seminary, Dayton, Ohio

"With ease, clarity, and care, the author lays out good news that no one should ignore. In this moment of world strife and uncertainty, a sure and better future lies within your grasp, starting right now. But how? Read this book to find out."

—Robert W. Yarbrough, Professor of New Testament, Covenant Theological Seminary, St. Louis, Missouri

"John 3:16 has become a confession of faith for many Christians. Wreh invites them into a conversation with scripture that will deepen their faith and help articulate what this passage means when explaining their faith to others. The questions at the end of each section help readers to explore what they find challenging and where their understandings are nuanced or varying. While adamant in his own convictions about the truth of John 3:16, Wreh's prose style is elegantly approachable, and his rhetoric is gentle and caring."

—Jo-Ann A. Brant, Professor Emerita, Goshen College

John 3:16

JOHN 3:16
God's Invitation to You

Resource Publications
An Imprint of Wipf and Stock Publishers
199 W. 8th Ave., Suite 3
Eugene, OR 97401

www.wipfandstock.com

PAPERBACK ISBN: 979-8-3852-7661-5
HARDCOVER ISBN: 979-8-3852-7662-2
EBOOK ISBN: 979-8-3852-7663-9

VERSION NUMBER 04/01/26

To every soul who has ever wondered,
"Is there more to life than this?"
This book is written for you.

To my wife, my faithful companion in ministry,
whose love reflects the love of Christ.

To my children, my greatest earthly joy,
who remind me daily why the gospel matters.

And to my Lord and Savior Jesus Christ,
who loved the world and gave Himself for it—
including me.

Contents

Preface: A Word to the Reader ix

Introduction: Why This Book? Why You? xi

PART ONE. THE GOD WHO LOVES

1 "For God . . . ": The One Who Initiates 3

2 " . . . So Loved . . . ": The Nature of Divine Love 14

3 " . . . The World . . . ": The Scope of God's Love 26

PART TWO. THE GIFT GOD GAVE

4 " . . . That He Gave . . . ": Love in Action 39

5 " . . . His Only Begotten Son . . . ": The Identity of the Gift 51

6 The Cross: What the Gift Cost 64

PART THREE. THE RESPONSE GOD REQUIRES

7 " . . . That Whoever Believes . . . ": What Faith Means 79

8 " . . . In Him . . . ": The Object of Faith 89

9 Repentance: The Other Side of Faith 103

PART FOUR. THE DESTINY GOD OFFERS

10 " . . . Shall Not Perish . . . ": The Judgment We Deserve 119

11 " . . . But Have Eternal Life": The Gift Beyond Imagination 130

12 What Eternal Life Looks Like: Now and Forever 137

PART FIVE. THE DECISION BEFORE YOU

13 Counting the Cost: What Following Jesus Requires 147

14 Common Obstacles: Answering the Objections 153

15 Today Is the Day: The Urgency of Belief 158

Epilogue: A Final Word of Hope 167

Appendix A: How to Study the Bible 171

Appendix B: Finding a Bible-Believing Church 175

Appendix C: Recommended Resources for New Believers 179

About the Author 187

Bibliography 189

Index 191

PREFACE

A Word to the Reader

Before you turn another page, I want to tell you something important: I did not write this book to argue with you.

I know that religious books can feel like debates—as if the author is trying to win a point, defeat an opponent, or prove someone wrong. That is not my intention. I have written this book because I genuinely believe that what the Bible says is true, and that if it is true, it is the most important truth you will ever encounter. I am not trying to defeat you; I am trying to introduce you to Someone who can transform you.

Let me tell you a little about myself. I was born in Liberia, West Africa, a nation that has known both beauty and brokenness. I have experienced war, displacement, loss, and suffering. I have also experienced the faithfulness of God through it all. My journey to faith was not easy or immediate. I had questions—hard questions—and I did not find Christianity compelling until I saw it lived out in people whose lives had been genuinely changed by Jesus Christ.

For over ten years, I have served as a pastor. I have sat with the dying and comforted the grieving. I have counseled the addicted and walked with the broken. I have preached at weddings and officiated at funerals. In all of this, I have seen one message transform lives like no other: the message of John 3:16—that God loves sinners, that He gave His Son to save them, and that whoever believes in Him will have eternal life.

This book is my attempt to share that message with you.

I write as a scholar. I have earned a Doctor of Ministry degree and am currently pursuing a PhD in Bible Exposition. I believe the Bible deserves careful study, and I will not insult your intelligence with shallow explanations. When I make a claim, I will support it from Scripture. When I encounter a difficult question, I will address it honestly.

But I also write as a pastor. I know that you are not merely a mind to be informed but a soul to be loved. The questions you bring to this book are not merely intellectual puzzles; they are matters of eternal significance. I will try to speak to your heart as well as your head.

Here is what I ask of you: Read with an open mind. You do not have to agree with everything I say, but I ask that you consider it fairly. If something I write troubles you, do not dismiss it immediately—wrestle with it. If something encourages you, do not brush it aside—embrace it. And if by the end of this book you find yourself drawn to believe in Jesus Christ, do not resist—respond.

I have prayed for you—yes, for you, the person holding this book right now. I do not know your name, your background, your struggles, or your doubts. But I have asked God to use these pages to speak to your soul. I believe He can. I believe He will.

So let us begin. Turn the page, and let me introduce you to the most famous verse in the world—and more importantly, to the God it reveals.

Dr. Elijah Wreh
LaGrange, Ohio
December 2025

INTRODUCTION

Why This Book? Why You?

"For God so loved the world, that He gave His only begotten Son, that whoever believes in Him shall not perish, but have eternal life."

— John 3:16 (NASB)

THE MOST FAMOUS VERSE IN THE WORLD

You have probably seen it before.

Maybe it was on a sign held up at a football game, visible for a split second on television before the camera moved on. Perhaps you noticed it on a bumper sticker while stuck in traffic, or spray-painted on an overpass, or printed on a coffee cup. "John 3:16"—three words and three numbers that have become one of the most recognized references in human history.

But what does it actually say? And more importantly, what does it mean?

John 3:16 is a single sentence from the Bible—twenty-five words in the original Greek, twenty-six in most English translations. The sixteenth-century German reformer Martin Luther called it "the gospel in miniature," because it compresses the entire message of Christianity into one compact statement. It tells you who God is, what God has done, what God requires, and what is at stake for your eternal soul.[1]

This book exists to unpack that sentence—to examine it word by word, phrase by phrase—and to explain why it matters more than anything else you will ever read.

WHO THIS BOOK IS WRITTEN FOR

This book is written for you—specifically for you—if you do not yet believe in Jesus Christ.

Perhaps you picked up this book out of curiosity. Maybe someone gave it to you—a friend, a family member, a colleague, a stranger. Perhaps you found it in a hotel room, a hospital waiting area, a coffee shop, or a used bookstore. However it came into your hands, I do not believe it was an accident. I believe God has placed this book before you for a reason.

You may identify as an atheist—someone who is convinced that God does not exist. You may be an agnostic—someone who is not sure whether God exists and doubts that anyone can know for certain. You may belong to another religion—Islam, Hinduism, Buddhism, Judaism, or something else—and wonder why Christians make such exclusive claims about Jesus. You may have grown up in a Christian home but never made the faith your own. You may have been hurt by the church or by people who claimed to follow Christ. You may be someone who has tried religion and found it empty, or someone who has avoided it entirely.

Wherever you are coming from, this book is for you.

I want to be clear about what this book is *not*. It is not a book trying to recruit you into a religion, a denomination, or a church membership program. It is not a book designed to make you a better person through moral improvement. It is not a book of religious platitudes or spiritual self-help advice.

1. Martin Luther called John 3:16 "the gospel in miniature" (das Evangelium im Kleinen). This phrase has been widely attributed to Luther in evangelical literature.

This book is an *invitation*—an invitation to meet a Person, to consider a claim, and to make a decision that will determine where you spend eternity.

WHY JOHN 3:16?

Of all the verses in the Bible—and there are over 31,000 of them—why focus an entire book on this one?

The answer is simple: because John 3:16 contains everything you need to know to be saved.

Consider what this single verse teaches:

- *"For God. . ."*—There is a God, and He is the starting point of everything.
- *". . .so loved. . ."*—This God is not distant or indifferent; He loves.
- *". . .the world. . ."*—His love extends to all humanity, including you.
- *". . .that He gave. . ."*—His love is not mere sentiment; it moved Him to action.
- *". . .His only begotten Son. . ."*—What He gave was infinitely precious: His unique Son, Jesus Christ.
- *". . .that whoever. . ."*—The offer is universal; no one is excluded from the invitation.
- *". . .believes in Him. . ."* The response required is faith—personal trust in Jesus.
- *". . .shall not perish. . ."*—Without Christ, the destiny is destruction; with Him, destruction is avoided.
- *". . .but have eternal life."*—The promise for believers is life that never ends.

In just twenty-six words, you have the character of God, the cost of salvation, the condition for receiving it, and the consequences of accepting or rejecting it. No other verse in the Bible packs so much into so little space.

THE PROBLEM OF FAMILIARITY

Here is the irony: John 3:16 is so famous that it has become invisible.

People see the reference—"John 3:16"—without ever reading the verse. They recognize the address without knowing what lives at that address. The bumper sticker has become so common that it registers as religious background noise rather than a life-changing message.

Even those who know the words often miss the meaning. They can recite the verse from memory without ever feeling its weight. "For God so loved the world. . ."—yes, yes, we know. But do we? Do we really understand what it means that the infinite, eternal, holy God loved a world in rebellion against Him? Do we grasp the scandal of the claim that He gave His own Son to die for sinners?

This book exists to break through the familiarity. I want to take words you may have heard a thousand times and help you hear them as if for the first time. I want to remove the religious veneer and show you the raw, stunning, terrifying, beautiful reality underneath.

WHAT THIS BOOK WILL DO

In the pages that follow, I will make a biblical and theological case for why you should believe in Jesus Christ. Let me tell you what to expect.

First, this book will take the Bible seriously. I will not ask you to accept claims without evidence. Everything I assert will be grounded in Scripture, and I will show you where. If you have a Bible, I encourage you to check my references. If you do not have a Bible, I will quote the relevant texts so you can see for yourself what they say. The early Christians in the city of Berea were commended because they "received the word with great eagerness, examining the Scriptures daily to see whether these things were so" (Acts 17:11). I invite you to do the same with this book.

Second, this book will take your questions seriously. I know you may have objections—serious objections. What about other religions? What about suffering? What about those who never hear the gospel? Is not Christianity intolerant and exclusive? How can anyone trust the Bible? These are not frivolous questions, and I will not treat them frivolously. In Chapter 13, I will address the most common objections directly and honestly.

Third, this book will take you seriously. I am not writing to a category of people called "unbelievers." I am writing to you—a real person with a real history, real struggles, real hopes, and real fears. I do not know your name, but God does. I do not know your story, but God does. And I believe He has brought this book into your life because He wants you to know Him.

HOW THIS BOOK IS ORGANIZED

The structure of this book follows the structure of John 3:16 itself. We will walk through the verse phrase by phrase, and each phrase will open up new vistas of understanding.

- *Part One: The God Who Loves* explores "For God so loved the world." We will ask: Who is this God? What does it mean that He loves? And who is included in His love?
- *Part Two: The Gift God Gave* explores "that He gave His only begotten Son." We will ask: Why was a gift necessary? Who is this Son? And what did His coming accomplish?
- *Part Three: The Response God Requires* explores "that whoever believes in Him." We will ask: What does it mean to believe? What is faith? And what role does repentance play?
- *Part Four: The Destiny God Offers* explores "shall not perish, but have eternal life." We will ask: What does it mean to perish? What is eternal life? And when does eternal life begin?

- *Part Five: The Decision Before You* brings everything together. We will address remaining objections, extend the invitation clearly, and guide you in your first steps if you choose to believe.

Each chapter concludes with questions for reflection. These are not academic exercises or discussion prompts for a study group. They are invitations to honest self-examination. I encourage you to take them seriously. Write your answers in a journal if that helps. The goal is not to finish this book but to be changed by its message.

THE STAKES

I want to be honest with you about what is at stake.

This is not a book about how to live a better life, find inner peace, or become a more moral person. Those things may happen as a result of what this book teaches, but they are not the main point. The main point is your eternal destiny.

John 3:16 presents two possible destinies: perishing or eternal life. There is no third option. According to Jesus—and He is the one speaking in John 3:16—every human being will experience one of these two outcomes. Either you will perish, which means facing the righteous judgment of God for your sins, or you will have eternal life, which means enjoying the presence and blessing of God forever.

The difference between these two destinies is belief in Jesus Christ. That is what John 3:16 says. "Whoever believes in Him shall not perish, but have eternal life." Belief is the hinge on which everything turns.

I am writing this book because I believe this is true. I am not playing a religious game. I am not trying to add members to my church or notches to my evangelistic belt. I am writing because I am convinced that Jesus Christ is the Son of God, that He died for sinners, that He rose from the dead, and that He offers eternal life to all who trust in Him. And I am convinced that you—whoever you are, wherever you are—need to hear this message and respond to it.

THE INVITATION

The Bible describes salvation as a gift (Ephesians 2:8–9). A gift, by definition, cannot be earned—it can only be received. God, through John 3:16, offers you the gift of eternal life through His Son Jesus Christ.

This book is my attempt to explain that gift clearly, to answer your questions about it honestly, and to invite you to receive it personally. The explanation and the answers are my responsibility. The receiving is yours.

I cannot make you believe. I would not want to, even if I could. Faith that is coerced is not faith. But I can present the case, address the obstacles, and extend the invitation. What you do with it is between you and God.

My prayer—and I have prayed for you, the reader of this book—is that by the time you reach the final page, you will not merely understand John 3:16 intellectually but believe it personally. And believing, you will have life in His name.

Welcome to the most important journey of your life.

Turn the page. Let us begin.

PART ONE

THE GOD WHO LOVES

"For God so loved the world . . . "

—John 3:16a

1

"For God . . . "

The One Who Initiates

"In the beginning God . . . "

—GENESIS 1:1

THE FIRST TWO WORDS

"For God."

Two words. Four letters in the original Greek: *Theos* (Θεός). And yet these two words carry more weight than entire libraries of human philosophy. Before we can understand love, before we can grasp the gift, before we can consider our response or contemplate our destiny, we must begin here—with God.[12]

John 3:16 does not begin with you. It does not begin with your needs, your questions, your spiritual journey, or your search for meaning. It begins with God. This is not an accident. This is the most important thing the verse wants you to understand: the story

1. Unless otherwise noted, all Scripture quotations are from the New American Standard Bible (NASB), 1995 update.

2. The Greek word for God is theos (θεός), appearing over 1,300 times in the New Testament.

of salvation does not start with humanity reaching up to God; it starts with God reaching down to humanity.

The Bible opens the same way: "In the beginning God created the heavens and the earth." Not "In the beginning, humans evolved" or "In the beginning, matter existed." The Bible's first word about ultimate reality is God. He is the starting point of everything—of creation, of history, of salvation, and of this verse.

If you are to understand John 3:16, you must understand who God is. Everything else flows from this.

DOES GOD EXIST?

Perhaps you are reading this as someone who is not sure God exists. Perhaps you consider yourself an atheist or an agnostic. If so, I appreciate your willingness to engage with a book that assumes God's existence. Let me briefly explain why I believe this assumption is reasonable.

The Bible, interestingly, never tries to prove God's existence through philosophical arguments. It simply declares him. "In the beginning God"—no preamble, no defense, no apology. The writers of Scripture assumed that God's existence was evident, and they were not wrong.

The apostle Paul, writing to the church in Rome, stated it this way: "For since the creation of the world His invisible attributes, His eternal power and divine nature, have been clearly seen, being understood through what has been made, so that they are without excuse." Paul's argument is simple: look at the world around you. The existence of creation points to a Creator. The design evident in nature points to a Designer. The order of the universe points to an intelligent Mind behind it.

Consider the complexity of a single human cell, containing more information than entire encyclopedias. Consider the fine-tuning of the universe—the precise values of physical constants that, if altered even slightly, would make life impossible. Consider the existence of consciousness, of moral intuition, of beauty, of love. Where do these things come from if there is no God?

The philosopher Blaise Pascal observed that there is a "God-shaped vacuum" in every human heart. We are restless, searching, longing for something more. We sense that we are made for something beyond this life. That intuition is not a delusion; it is a signpost pointing to the One who made us.[3]

I will not pretend that these brief paragraphs settle the question of God's existence. Volumes have been written on this subject, and I encourage you to explore it further. But I ask you to consider: What if God is real? What if the Bible's opening declaration is true? What would that mean for your life, your choices, your destiny?

John 3:16 invites you to find out.

WHAT KIND OF GOD?

But it is not enough to believe that a god exists. The question is: What kind of God? The word "god" means different things to different people. To the ancient Greeks, the gods were powerful but petty, capable of jealousy and cruelty. To the deist, God is a distant clockmaker who wound up the universe and walked away. To the pantheist, God is an impersonal force permeating everything. To the Muslim, Allah is absolutely sovereign but unknowable in personal intimacy.

The God of John 3:16 is none of these.

When the Bible says "God," it refers to a very specific Being with very specific attributes. Let me introduce you to the God of Scripture—the God who "so loved the world."

God Is Personal

The God of the Bible is not an impersonal force or abstract principle. He is a Person—or more precisely, three Persons in one God: Father, Son, and Holy Spirit. This is the doctrine of the Trinity,

3. Blaise Pascal, Pensées, trans. A. J. Krailsheimer (London: Penguin, 1966), fragment 148. The exact phrase "God-shaped vacuum" is a paraphrase of Pascal's argument.

which we will explore more fully when we discuss "His only begotten Son" in chapter 5.

For now, the crucial point is this: God is personal. He thinks. He wills. He feels. He speaks. He acts. He relates. Throughout Scripture, God reveals himself as One who enters into relationship with his creatures. He walks with Adam in the garden. He speaks to Abraham as a friend. He wrestles with Jacob. He reveals his name to Moses. He grieves over Israel's unfaithfulness.

This is revolutionary. Many religions offer a god who is distant, unknowable, unapproachable. The Bible offers a God who desires relationship with the people he has made. John 3:16 is itself evidence of this personal nature—a personal God who personally loves and personally gives.

God Is Eternal

> *"Before the mountains were born or You gave birth to the earth and the world, even from everlasting to everlasting, You are God."* (Ps 90:2)

God has no beginning and no end. He was not created; he simply is. When Moses asked God his name, God responded, "I AM WHO I AM"—a declaration of self-existence, of being that depends on nothing outside itself.

This means God is not subject to time. He does not grow old or change with the ages. "Jesus Christ is the same yesterday and today and forever." The God who loved the world two thousand years ago loves the world today with the same eternal, unchanging love.

God Is All-Powerful

> *"Ah Lord GOD! Behold, You have made the heavens and the earth by Your great power and by Your outstretched arm! Nothing is too difficult for You."* (Jer 32:17)

The technical term is "omnipotence"—God is all-powerful. He spoke the universe into existence. He sustains every atom by the word of his power. He raises the dead, calms the storms, and overrules the plans of nations. There is no limit to what he can do.

This matters for John 3:16 because it means God's love is not impotent. When God decides to save, he has the power to accomplish it. The gift he gave—his Son—was not a desperate gamble but a sovereign act of omnipotent love.

God Is All-Knowing

> *"Great is our Lord and abundant in strength; His understanding is infinite."* (Ps 147:5)

God knows everything—past, present, and future. He knows every thought in every mind, every motive in every heart, every word before it is spoken. He knows you completely—your secrets, your sins, your fears, your hopes. "You know when I sit down and when I rise up; You understand my thought from afar," David wrote. "Even before there is a word on my tongue, behold, O LORD, You know it all."

This is both terrifying and comforting. Terrifying, because nothing is hidden from God. You cannot deceive him, impress him with pretense, or hide your true self from his gaze. Comforting, because when John 3:16 says God loved "the world," he knew exactly what he was loving. He loved with full knowledge of how broken, rebellious, and sinful the world is. His love is not based on ignorance of your faults; it exists in spite of full awareness of them.

God Is Everywhere Present

> *"Where can I go from Your Spirit? Or where can I flee from Your presence? If I ascend to heaven, You are there; if I make my bed in Sheol, behold, You are there."* (Ps 139:7–8)

God is omnipresent—present everywhere at once. He is not confined to temples, churches, or sacred spaces. He is not limited to certain regions or religions. Wherever you are right now, as you read these words, God is there. He is not far from any one of us.

This means you do not need to go on a pilgrimage to find God. You do not need to climb a mountain, enter a cathedral, or travel to a holy land. God is present with you right now, this very moment, in whatever room or space you occupy. The invitation of John 3:16 is extended to you where you are.

God Is Holy

> *"Holy, Holy, Holy, is the LORD of hosts, the whole earth is full of His glory."* (Isa 6:3)

Holiness is the attribute that sets God apart from everything else. It means he is absolutely pure, completely without sin, utterly righteous. In the presence of God's holiness, the seraphim—angelic beings of immense power—cover their faces and cry out in worship. When the prophet Isaiah glimpsed God's holiness, he cried, "Woe is me, for I am ruined! Because I am a man of unclean lips."

God's holiness is why sin is such a serious problem. A holy God cannot simply ignore sin or pretend it does not matter. His righteousness demands justice. This creates a dilemma: How can a holy God have a relationship with unholy people?

John 3:16 is the answer to that dilemma. But we are getting ahead of ourselves. For now, remember this: the God who "so loved the world" is the thrice-holy God before whom angels veil their faces. His love is not the indulgence of a grandfather who winks at wrongdoing. It is the holy love of a righteous God who found a way to save sinners without compromising his holiness.

God Is Just

> *"Righteousness and justice are the foundation of Your throne."* (Ps 89:14)

Because God is holy, he is also just. He does not pervert justice. He does not let the guilty go unpunished or punish the innocent. Every wrong will be made right. Every injustice will be addressed. Every sin will be dealt with.

This is good news when we think about the evils of the world—the oppression, the cruelty, the injustice that often seems to go unpunished. God sees. God remembers. God will judge.

But it is sobering news when we think about ourselves. If God is just, and if we have sinned—and we have—then we face judgment. "The wages of sin is death." "The soul who sins will die." A just God cannot simply overlook our rebellion.

This brings us to the heart of John 3:16. How can a just God save sinners without being unjust? How can he forgive without ignoring sin? The answer is in the gift he gave—but again, we are getting ahead of ourselves.

GOD TAKES THE INITIATIVE

"For God . . . "

Notice what the verse does not say. It does not say, "For humanity searched for God" or "For people tried hard enough" or "For religious seekers finally found the truth." It says, "For God." God is the subject of the sentence. God is the one acting. God is the initiator.

This is one of the most important truths in all of Scripture: salvation begins with God, not with us.

Many people think of religion as humanity's search for God. We climb the mountain seeking the divine. We perform rituals hoping to gain God's favor. We try different paths, different practices, different beliefs, hoping one of them will lead us to enlightenment or salvation.

The Bible turns this completely upside down. The story of Scripture is not humanity searching for God; it is God searching for humanity. From the very beginning, when Adam and Eve sinned and hid themselves in the garden, it was God who came looking: "Where are you?" God initiated. God sought. God called.

This pattern continues throughout the Bible:

God called Abraham out of a pagan land and made him the father of a nation.

God appeared to Moses in a burning bush and sent him to deliver Israel.

God sent prophets to call his people back when they strayed.

God sent his own Son into the world to save it (John 3:16).

Jesus himself said, "No one can come to Me unless the Father who sent Me draws him." The initiative belongs to God. Before you ever thought about seeking God, God was seeking you.

WHY THIS MATTERS

Why does it matter that God initiates?

First, it removes the burden from your shoulders. If salvation depended on your ability to find God, to figure out the right path, to climb high enough—you would be hopeless. How could finite, fallen, limited human beings ever reach the infinite, holy, transcendent God? You could not. But you do not have to. God has come to you.

Second, it demonstrates God's love. Why would God bother? Why would the eternal, self-sufficient, all-powerful Creator care about creatures who have rebelled against him? He did not have to. He chose to. That choice reveals his heart.

Third, it ensures that salvation is available to everyone. If salvation depended on human effort, intelligence, or spiritual achievement, only the elite would make it. But because God initiates, salvation is offered to all—the wise and the foolish, the strong and the weak, the religious and the irreligious. "Whoever believes" has access, because God has made access possible.

Fourth, it means God is at work even now. If you are reading this book and sensing something stirring in your heart—a curiosity, a hunger, a conviction—that is not random. God may be drawing you to himself. The fact that this book is in your hands may be part of his initiative in your life.

THE GOD BEHIND JOHN 3:16

Let me bring together what we have learned.

The God of John 3:16 is not a vague, generic deity. He is the specific God revealed in the pages of Scripture:

He is personal—capable of relationship, capable of love.

He is eternal—his love is not temporary or fleeting.

He is all-powerful—his love is backed by infinite ability to save.

He is all-knowing—his love is given with full awareness of who we are.

He is everywhere present—his love reaches you wherever you are.

He is holy—his love does not compromise his purity.

He is just—his love satisfies the demands of righteousness.

And this God—this infinite, eternal, holy God—initiated. He moved first. He loved. He gave.

This is the God who is inviting you through John 3:16. He is not a concept to be debated but a Person to be encountered. He is not far away, hoping you will find him; he is near, reaching out his hand.

A WORD TO THE SKEPTIC

Perhaps you have read this chapter with a degree of skepticism. You are not yet convinced that this God exists, or that the Bible accurately describes him. I understand. These are not small claims.

Let me offer you a challenge: Keep reading.

You do not have to believe everything in this chapter to continue the journey. Consider it a hypothesis to be tested. If the God of John 3:16 is real, the evidence should become clearer as we proceed. If his love is genuine, the proof will be in what he did.

In the next chapter, we will examine the second phrase: "so loved." We will ask what kind of love this is and why it matters. The character of God will become even clearer.

For now, I ask only this: Be open. The God who initiates may be initiating right now—through these very words.

QUESTIONS FOR REFLECTION

- Before reading this chapter, what was your view of God? Has anything shifted or been clarified?
- Which of God's attributes—personal, eternal, all-powerful, all-knowing, everywhere present, holy, just—is most striking to you? Why?
- How does it change things to know that God initiates salvation rather than waiting for us to find him?
- If God is truly all-knowing, he knows everything about you—your past, your secrets, your thoughts. How does that make you feel?
- Do you sense that God might be "initiating" something in your life by bringing this book to you? Explain.

A PRAYER

God, if you are real—and I am beginning to think you might be—I ask you to reveal yourself to me. I do not have all the answers, and I am not sure what I believe. But I am willing to search. Open my eyes to see you as you truly are. Help me understand the message of John

3:16. If you are the God who initiates, then initiate in my life. Draw me to yourself. I am listening.

Amen.

2

" . . . So Loved . . . "

The Nature of Divine Love

"God is love."

—1 John 4:8

THE MOST MISUNDERSTOOD WORD

"For God so loved . . . "

Love. No word in the English language carries more weight or creates more confusion. We use the same word to describe our feelings about pizza, our affection for a pet, our devotion to a spouse, and God's disposition toward the world. The result is that when we hear "God so loved the world," we instinctively pour into that word whatever meaning we already associate with love—and we almost always get it wrong.

The original language of the New Testament is Greek, and the Greek word used in John 3:16 is *agapaō* (ἀγαπάω). This is not the only Greek word for love. The ancient Greeks had at least four distinct terms, each describing a different kind of affection.

Understanding these distinctions will help us grasp just how remarkable it is that God "loved" the world.[1]

FOUR GREEK WORDS FOR LOVE

C. S. Lewis, in his classic book *The Four Loves*, explored the different dimensions of love recognized in ancient thought. While the categories overlap and the distinctions are not always rigid, understanding them illuminates what the Bible means when it says God "loved" the world.[2]

Storgē—Affection

Storgē (στοργή) is the love of natural affection—the bond between parents and children, the fondness we develop for familiar people and places. It is comfortable, warm, and often taken for granted. A mother's instinctive care for her infant, a child's attachment to home, the affection between old friends—these are expressions of *storgē*.

This is not the word used in John 3:16. God's love for the world is not merely natural affection or comfortable familiarity. It is something far deeper.

Philia—Friendship

Philia (φιλία) is the love of friendship—the bond between companions who share common interests, values, or experiences. It is the camaraderie of soldiers, the kinship of fellow scholars, the loyalty between those who have chosen each other as friends. *Philia* is mutual; it exists between equals who delight in each other's company.

This is not the word used in John 3:16 either. God's love for the world is not based on mutual affection or shared interests. The world did not befriend God; it rebelled against him. Yet he loved it still.

1. The Greek verb agapaō (ἀγαπάω) and its cognate noun agapē (ἀγάπη) became the characteristic New Testament term for divine love.

2. C. S. Lewis, The Four Loves (New York: Harcourt, 1960), 17–38.

Erōs—Romantic Love

Erōs (ἔρως) is romantic, passionate love—the desire to possess and be united with the beloved. It is the love celebrated in poetry and songs, the intoxicating attraction that draws two people together. *Erōs* seeks fulfillment; it loves because the beloved is beautiful, desirable, and satisfying.

This word never appears in the New Testament. God's love is not driven by desire for what we can give him. He does not love us because we are beautiful or because we complete him. He is entirely self-sufficient. His love flows from his own character, not from our attractiveness.

Agapē—Self-Giving Love

Agapē (ἀγάπη) is the word the New Testament writers chose to describe God's love—and their choice was deliberate. In classical Greek, *agapē* was a relatively colorless word, lacking the emotional intensity of *erōs* or the warmth of *philia*. But the biblical writers filled it with new meaning. They used *agapē* to describe a love that is:

Unconditional—not based on the worthiness of the beloved

Self-giving—willing to sacrifice for the good of the beloved

Initiating—not a response to being loved first

Unchanging—not fluctuating with circumstances or emotions

This is the love of John 3:16. When the Bible says "God so loved the world," it uses *agapē*—a love that gives without expecting return, a love that reaches out to the undeserving, a love that persists even when rejected.

GOD IS LOVE

The apostle John makes an astonishing claim: "God is love." Notice that he does not merely say God *has* love, as if love were one attribute among many. He says God *is* love. Love is not something God does occasionally; it is who he is essentially.

This does not mean that love is God—that would be to make an abstract concept into a deity. Rather, it means that God's nature is perfectly loving. Everything he does flows from love. His creation was an act of love. His commands are expressions of love. His judgments are consistent with love. His salvation is the supreme demonstration of love.

Before time began, within the Trinity itself, there was love. The Father has eternally loved the Son. The Son has eternally loved the Father. The Spirit has eternally been the bond of that love. God did not create the world because he was lonely or needed someone to love. He created out of the overflow of the love that has always existed within his own being.

When John 3:16 says "God so loved the world," it is telling you that the God whose very nature is love turned his attention toward you.

LOVE THAT MOVES FIRST

One of the most remarkable features of God's love is that it initiates. It moves first. It does not wait to be loved before loving.

> *"But God demonstrates His own love toward us, in that while we were yet sinners, Christ died for us."* (Rom 5:8)

Did you catch that? *While we were yet sinners.* Not after we cleaned up our act. Not once we became lovable. Not when we started seeking God. While we were still in rebellion, still running from him, still shaking our fists at heaven—that is when God loved us. That is when Christ died for us.

> *"But God, being rich in mercy, because of His great love with which He loved us, even when we were dead in our transgressions, made us alive together with Christ."* (Eph 2:4–5)

Even when we were dead. A dead person cannot do anything to make themselves lovable. A corpse cannot reach out to God. Yet

God, because of his great love, reached out to us while we were spiritually lifeless and made us alive.

This is radically different from human love. Human love is typically responsive—we love those who love us, who are kind to us, who meet our needs, who are attractive to us. God's love is initiative—he loves first, loves the undeserving, loves those who have nothing to offer him in return.

LOVE THAT IS NOT EARNED

If there is one thing that distinguishes *agapē* love from every other kind, it is this: it is not based on the worthiness of the beloved.

Consider how God describes his love for Israel:

> *"The LORD did not set His love on you nor choose you because you were more in number than any of the peoples, for you were the fewest of all peoples, but because the LORD loved you."* (Deut 7:7–8)

Notice the circular reasoning: Why did God love Israel? Because he loved them. There is no external cause, no reason outside of God himself. He did not choose them because they were impressive, numerous, or righteous. He chose them because he chose to love them. His love originates in his own character, not in the attractiveness of the beloved.

The same is true of his love for you. God does not love you because you are lovable. He does not love you because of your good works, your moral achievements, your religious efforts, or your potential. He loves you because he is love. The cause of his love is in him, not in you.

This is either the most liberating or the most offensive truth you will ever hear. It is liberating because it means you do not have to earn God's love—you cannot earn it, and you do not need to. It is already freely given. It is offensive because it strips away all pretense of self-worth. You bring nothing to the table that causes God to love you. His love is pure grace.

LOVE THAT PURSUES

The prophet Hosea was given a painful assignment: marry a woman who would be unfaithful to him, so that his life would become a living parable of God's love for his unfaithful people.

> *"I have loved you with an everlasting love; therefore I have drawn you with lovingkindness."* (Jer 31:3)

Through Hosea, God reveals himself as a husband pursuing an adulterous wife, a father longing for a rebellious child:

> *"When Israel was a youth I loved him, and out of Egypt I called My son."* (Hos 11:1)
>
> *"How can I give you up, O Ephraim? How can I surrender you, O Israel? . . . My heart is turned over within Me, all My compassions are kindled."* (Hos 11:8)

Do you hear the ache in God's voice? This is not a cold, philosophical love. This is the burning passion of a lover who cannot let go, a father whose heart breaks over his wayward children. God pursues. He does not give up. Even when his people run from him, he runs after them.

And then comes the most shocking command: Hosea is told to go and buy back his unfaithful wife, who has left him for other lovers and ended up a slave. He is to redeem her, restore her, love her again. Why? Because that is exactly what God does for his people. That is what God does for you.

LOVE THAT SACRIFICES

The ultimate proof of love is sacrifice. Jesus himself said, "Greater love has no one than this, that one lay down his life for his friends." By that measure, the love of John 3:16 is the greatest love ever demonstrated.

"For God so loved the world, that He *gave* . . . " The love described here is not merely feeling; it is action. It is not sentiment; it is sacrifice. God did not merely feel affection for the world from a safe distance. He gave. He entered into our suffering. He paid a price.

> *"In this is love, not that we loved God, but that He loved us and sent His Son to be the propitiation for our sins."* (1 John 4:10)

The word "propitiation" may be unfamiliar, but its meaning is crucial. It refers to a sacrifice that turns away wrath, that satisfies the demands of justice. God's love did not ignore his holiness; it satisfied it. His love found a way to forgive sinners without pretending sin did not matter. He sent his Son to bear the penalty we deserved.

We will explore this more fully in chapter 6 when we examine the cross. For now, simply note this: the love of God is costly love. It is not cheap sentiment. It is blood-bought, death-defying, sacrifice-making love.

BUT WHAT ABOUT THE WORLD?

Here is what makes John 3:16 truly astonishing: the object of God's love is "the world." The Greek word is *kosmos* (κόσμος), and in John's writings, it often refers not just to the created order but to humanity in its rebellion against God.[3]

God did not love a world that loved him back. He loved a world that:

Was his *enemy*: "For if while we were enemies we were reconciled to God through the death of His Son, much more, having been reconciled, we shall be saved by His life."

Was *dead in sin*: "And you were dead in your trespasses and sins, in which you formerly walked according to the course of this world."

Was *hostile in mind*: "And although you were formerly alienated and hostile in mind, engaged in evil deeds."

3. The Greek word kosmos (κόσμος) appears 78 times in John's Gospel, more than in any other New Testament book.

Was *separated from God*: "But your iniquities have made a separation between you and your God."

This is the world God loved. Not a world of innocent victims. Not a world of sincere seekers. A world of rebels, enemies, corpses, and fugitives. A world that had turned its back on its Creator and exchanged his glory for idols.

And God loved it anyway.

THE SCANDAL OF DIVINE LOVE

Let me be direct about who you are, according to the Bible, so that you can understand just how remarkable God's love is.

You are a sinner. "For all have sinned and fall short of the glory of God." This is not a harsh judgment from a religious fanatic. This is a diagnosis from the Great Physician. Every human being has rebelled against God, violated his law, fallen short of his standard.

"There is none righteous, not even one; there is none who understands, there is none who seeks for God; all have turned aside, together they have become useless." This is the human condition. We are not basically good people who occasionally make mistakes. We are fundamentally broken people whose very nature is bent toward sin.

The Bible describes our hearts as "only evil continually," "deceitful above all things and desperately wicked," and says we are sinful from conception. We are described as "by nature children of wrath."

This is not pleasant to hear. But it is essential to understand if you are to grasp the magnitude of God's love. He did not love us because we were worthy. He loved us in spite of our unworthiness. He loved enemies. He loved rebels. He loved sinners.

He loved you.

LOVE AND WRATH

At this point, you may be confused. If God is love, why does the Bible also speak of God's wrath? How can the same God who "so loved the world" also be a God of judgment?

The answer is that love and wrath are not opposites—they are two sides of the same coin.

Consider: if you love something, you must hate whatever destroys it. A mother who loves her child will be furious at anyone who harms that child. A doctor who loves health must hate disease. A judge who loves justice must hate injustice.

God loves righteousness, so he hates sin. God loves his creatures, so he hates what destroys them. God loves his glory, so he hates whatever dishonors it. His wrath is not a contradiction of his love; it is an expression of it.

"He who believes in the Son has eternal life; but he who does not obey the Son will not see life, but the wrath of God abides on him." "For the wrath of God is revealed from heaven against all ungodliness and unrighteousness of men."

Here is the tension at the heart of John 3:16: the God who loves the world is also the God whose wrath rests on sinners. How can both be true? How can a holy God love unholy people without compromising his holiness? The answer is in what he gave—his only begotten Son. But that is the subject of our next chapter.

WHAT "SO LOVED" REALLY MEANS

"For God *so* loved the world." That little word "so" is easily overlooked, but it carries profound meaning. In Greek, the word is *houtōs* (οὕτως), and it can mean either "so much" (indicating degree) or "in this way" (indicating manner).

Both meanings are true. God loved the world *so much* that he gave his Son. And God loved the world *in this way*—by giving his Son. The depth of his love is demonstrated by the nature of his gift.

You cannot measure love by words. "I love you" is easy to say. You measure love by sacrifice. What is someone willing to give up for you? What price are they willing to pay? By that measure, God's love is immeasurable. He gave his only Son. There is no greater gift. There is no higher price.

THIS LOVE IS FOR YOU

Perhaps you have read this chapter thinking, "This sounds wonderful, but surely it cannot apply to me. You do not know what I've done. You do not know who I really am."

You're right—I do not. But God does. He knows every sin you've committed, every thought you've entertained, every secret you've hidden. And here is the staggering truth: he loved you before you did any of those things. He loved you knowing you would do them. He loves you still.

> *"See how great a love the Father has bestowed on us, that we would be called children of God."* (1 John 3:1)

The Father does not merely tolerate you. He does not grudgingly accept you. He *bestows great love* on you. He invites you to become his child.

> *"The LORD your God is in your midst, a victorious warrior.*
> *He will exult over you with joy, He will be quiet in His love,*
> *He will rejoice over you with shouts of joy."* (Zeph 3:17)

Can you imagine it? God *rejoicing* over you. God *exulting* over you. God shouting for joy because of you. This is not cold, distant deity. This is a Father who delights in his children.

> *"Just as a father has compassion on his children, so the LORD has compassion on those who fear Him."* (Ps 103:13)
> *"Can a woman forget her nursing child and have no compassion on the son of her womb? Even these may forget, but I will not forget you. Behold, I have inscribed you on the palms of My hands."* (Isa 49:15–16)

Your name is inscribed on the palms of God's hands. A mother might forget her infant—but God will never forget you. His love is more constant than the most primal human bond.

> *"For I am convinced that neither death, nor life, nor angels, nor principalities, nor things present, nor things to come, nor powers, nor height, nor depth, nor any other created thing, will be able to separate us from the love of God, which is in Christ Jesus our Lord."* (Rom 8:38–39)

Nothing can separate you from this love. Not death. Not life. Not angels or demons. Not present circumstances or future fears. Not the heights of success or the depths of failure. Nothing in all creation. If you are in Christ, you are loved with an unbreakable, unshakeable, eternal love.

QUESTIONS FOR REFLECTION

- Before reading this chapter, what did you think "love" meant when applied to God? Has your understanding changed?
- Which aspect of God's *agapē* love is most difficult for you to accept—that it is unconditional, that it pursues you, that it required sacrifice, or that it is for sinners?
- How does it make you feel to know that God loved you "while you were yet a sinner"—not after you improved?
- Do you find the Bible's description of human sinfulness offensive? Why or why not? How does understanding your sinfulness affect your appreciation of God's love?
- Have you ever felt unloved or unlovable? How does the message of this chapter speak to that experience?

A PRAYER

God, I am beginning to see that your love is different from anything I have known. It does not wait for me to earn it. It does not depend on my worthiness. It reaches out to me even though I have turned away from you. I confess that I am the sinner described in this chapter—rebellious, broken, undeserving. And yet you love me. Help me to believe this. Help me to receive this love. Show me more of who you are, and help me to respond with faith.

Amen.

3

" . . . The World . . . "

The Scope of God's Love

"After these things I looked, and behold, a great multitude which no one could count, from every nation and all tribes and peoples and tongues, standing before the throne."

—Revelation 7:9

A SMALL WORD WITH VAST IMPLICATIONS

"For God so loved the world . . . "

The world. In Greek, *kosmos* (κόσμος). It is a small word, easily passed over, but its implications are staggering. When John wrote that God loved "the world," he was making a claim that would have shocked many of his original readers—and should still astonish us today.

Who, exactly, did God love? A select group of religious insiders? A particular nation? Those who had already proven themselves worthy? No. God loved the *world*—the entire rebellious, broken, sinful mass of humanity. Every tribe. Every tongue. Every nation. Every individual, without exception.

This includes you.

WHAT DOES "WORLD" MEAN?

The word *kosmos* appears more frequently in John's writings than anywhere else in the New Testament. John uses this word with several different nuances, and understanding them helps us grasp what he means in John 3:16.

The Created Order

Sometimes *kosmos* refers to the physical universe—the created order that God brought into being. John writes that "the world was made through Him," referring to Jesus Christ. Jesus speaks of the glory he had with the Father "before the world was." In this sense, "world" simply means the cosmos—the heavens and the earth and everything in them.

Humanity in General

More often in John's writings, *kosmos* refers specifically to humanity—the world of people. When John the Baptist sees Jesus and declares, "Behold, the Lamb of God who takes away the sin of the world," he is not talking about rocks and trees. He is talking about human beings. When the Samaritans call Jesus "the Savior of the world," they mean he is the Savior of all people. When Jesus says, "I am the bread of life" that "gives life to the world," he is offering himself to humanity.

Humanity in Rebellion

But John often uses *kosmos* with a darker connotation: the world as a system organized in opposition to God. The "ruler of this world" is Satan. The world "hates" Jesus and his followers. Believers are warned not to "love the world" because "all that is in the world, the lust of the flesh and the lust of the eyes and the boastful pride of life, is not from the Father, but is from the world."

This is the world of John 3:16—not merely the physical planet, but *humanity in its fallenness*. The world that God loved is the world that had turned its back on him. The world that God loved is the world under the dominion of the evil one. The world that God loved is you and me and every other human being who has ever lived—all of us rebels, all of us sinners, all of us in desperate need of rescue.

This is what makes God's love so extraordinary. He did not love a world that was seeking him. He loved a world that was running from him. He did not love a world that deserved his affection. He loved a world that deserved his judgment.

GOD'S GLOBAL PURPOSE FROM THE BEGINNING

Some people mistakenly believe that God was only interested in one nation—Israel—until Jesus came along and opened things up to everyone else. This misses the entire trajectory of Scripture. From the very beginning, God's plan was global.

When God called Abraham, he made this promise:

> *"Go forth from your country, and from your relatives and from your father's house, to the land which I will show you; and I will make you a great nation, and I will bless you, and make your name great; and so you shall be a blessing; and I will bless those who bless you, and the one who curses you I will curse. And in you all the families of the earth will be blessed."* (Gen 12:1–3)

Did you catch that? "*All the families of the earth* will be blessed." God chose Abraham not because he wanted to bless only Abraham's descendants, but because through Abraham's descendants, he intended to bless everyone. The promise was repeated and expanded: "In your seed all the nations of the earth shall be blessed."

Israel was chosen not as an exclusive recipient of God's love but as a channel through which that love would flow to all nations.

They were to be "a kingdom of priests and a holy nation"—mediators between God and the world.

THE PROPHETS SAW IT COMING

The Old Testament prophets repeatedly spoke of a day when God's salvation would extend beyond Israel to embrace the nations.

Isaiah proclaimed that God's Servant would be "a light to the nations" so that God's "salvation may reach to the end of the earth." He envisioned God's house as "a house of prayer for all the peoples."

The psalmist prayed:

> *"God be gracious to us and bless us, and cause His face to shine upon us—that Your way may be known on the earth, Your salvation among all nations."* (Ps 67:1–2)

Even the reluctant prophet Jonah was sent to preach to Nineveh—the capital of Israel's enemy, Assyria—because God cared about those 120,000 people "who do not know the difference between their right and left hand." Amos declared that God's concern extended beyond Israel: "Are you not as the sons of Ethiopia to Me, O sons of Israel?" declares the LORD. "Have I not brought up Israel from the land of Egypt, and the Philistines from Caphtor and the Arameans from Kir?"

God's love has always been global in scope. John 3:16 is not an innovation; it is the fulfillment of what God promised from the beginning.

JESUS AND THE OUTSIDERS

When Jesus walked the earth, his ministry was a living demonstration that God's love extends to all people—including those whom the religious establishment had written off.

Consider the woman at the well in John 4. She was a Samaritan—a member of a people group that Jews despised. The animosity between Jews and Samaritans was so intense that "Jews have no dealings with Samaritans." They would go miles out of their way to avoid Samaritan territory. They considered Samaritans religious half-breeds, unclean, outside the covenant.

But Jesus went straight through Samaria. He sat down at a well and struck up a conversation with a Samaritan woman—something no respectable rabbi would do. He offered her "living water." He revealed himself as the Messiah. And then he said something revolutionary:

> *"Woman, believe Me, an hour is coming when neither in this mountain nor in Jerusalem will you worship the Father . . . But an hour is coming, and now is, when the true worshipers will worship the Father in spirit and truth."* (John 4:21, 23)

Jesus was declaring that the old divisions were coming to an end. Worship would no longer be limited to Jerusalem or to Jews. True worshipers from every background would come to the Father. The result? Many Samaritans believed, declaring, "This is indeed the Savior of the world."

The Savior of the *world*. Not just the Savior of Israel. The *kosmos*.

THE GREAT COMMISSION

During his earthly ministry, Jesus focused primarily on Israel. But after his resurrection, he made God's global intention explicit:

> *"Go therefore and make disciples of all the nations, baptizing them in the name of the Father and the Son and the Holy Spirit."* (Matt 28:19)
> *"You will receive power when the Holy Spirit has come upon you; and you shall be My witnesses both in Jerusalem, and in all Judea and Samaria, and even to the remotest part of the earth."* (Acts 1:8)

All nations. The remotest part of the earth. The scope of God's love, demonstrated in John 3:16, would now be proclaimed to everyone everywhere.

THE WALL COMES DOWN

The book of Acts records the explosive expansion of the gospel beyond Jewish boundaries. It was not an easy transition. Many early believers struggled to accept that Gentiles—non-Jews—could be included in God's people without first becoming Jews.

The turning point came when the apostle Peter was sent to the home of a Roman centurion named Cornelius. Peter had to overcome his own prejudices even to enter a Gentile's house. But when he saw the Holy Spirit fall on Cornelius and his household, he declared:

> *"I most certainly understand now that God is not one to show partiality, but in every nation the man who fears Him and does what is right is welcome to Him."* (Acts 10:34–35)

God is not one to show partiality. This was revolutionary. The Jewish believers who witnessed it were "amazed" that "the gift of the Holy Spirit had been poured out on the Gentiles also." When Peter reported back to the church in Jerusalem, they glorified God, saying, "Well then, God has granted to the Gentiles also the repentance that leads to life."

The apostle Paul would later write that Christ "is our peace, who made both groups into one and broke down the barrier of the dividing wall." He reminded Gentile believers:

> *"Remember that you were at that time separate from Christ, excluded from the commonwealth of Israel, and strangers to the covenants of promise, having no hope and without God in the world. But now in Christ Jesus you who formerly were far off have been brought near by the blood of Christ."* (Eph 2:12–13)

"You who formerly were far off have been brought near." This is what John 3:16 means in practice. God loved the world—including those who were "far off," excluded, strangers, without hope. And through Christ, they have been brought near.

NEITHER JEW NOR GREEK

In Christ, the old divisions that separated humanity have been overcome:

> *"There is neither Jew nor Greek, there is neither slave nor free man, there is neither male nor female; for you are all one in Christ Jesus."* (Gal 3:28)

This does not mean that differences disappear. Jews are still Jews. Greeks are still Greeks. Men are still men. Women are still women. But these differences no longer determine our standing before God. In Christ, all who believe have equal access to the Father. All are equally loved. All are equally welcomed.

The vision of Revelation shows us the ultimate fulfillment of God's global love:

> *"Worthy are You to take the book and to break its seals; for You were slain, and purchased for God with Your blood men from every tribe and tongue and people and nation."* (Rev 5:9)

> *"After these things I looked, and behold, a great multitude which no one could count, from every nation and all tribes and peoples and tongues, standing before the throne and before the Lamb, clothed in white robes, and palm branches were in their hands; and they cry out with a loud voice, saying, 'Salvation to our God who sits on the throne, and to the Lamb.'"* (Rev 7:9–10)

A great multitude that no one could count. From *every nation*. All *tribes*. All *peoples*. All *tongues*. This is what "God so loved the world" looks like in its final fulfillment—a redeemed humanity from every corner of the earth, united in worship of the Lamb who was slain.

THE GOSPEL IS FOR ALL

The New Testament repeatedly emphasizes that the gospel—the good news of salvation through Jesus Christ—is for everyone:

> *"For I am not ashamed of the gospel, for it is the power of God for salvation to everyone who believes, to the Jew first and also to the Greek."* (Rom 1:16)
>
> *"For there is no distinction between Jew and Greek; for the same Lord is Lord of all, abounding in riches for all who call on Him; for 'Whoever will call on the name of the Lord will be saved.'"* (Rom 10:12–13)
>
> *"This is good and acceptable in the sight of God our Savior, who desires all men to be saved and to come to the knowledge of the truth."* (1 Tim 2:3–4)
>
> *"The Lord is not slow about His promise, as some count slowness, but is patient toward you, not wishing for any to perish but for all to come to repentance."* (2 Pet 3:9)
>
> *"For the grace of God has appeared, bringing salvation to all men."* (Titus 2:11)
>
> *"And He Himself is the propitiation for our sins; and not for ours only, but also for those of the whole world."* (1 John 2:2)

The testimony of Scripture is unanimous: God's love extends to the whole world. His desire is for all people to be saved. His grace has appeared for all. Christ died for the sins of the whole world.

WHAT ABOUT YOU?

Perhaps you have been reading this chapter wondering where you fit in. Let me be direct: you are part of "the world" that God loved.

It does not matter what nation you come from. God loved the world—including your nation.

It does not matter what language you speak. God loved the world—including speakers of your language.

It does not matter what your ethnic background is. God loved the world—including your people group.

It does not matter what your social status is. God loved the world—rich and poor, educated and uneducated, powerful and marginalized.

It does not matter what your past is. God loved the world—including those with shameful histories, criminal records, broken relationships, and wasted years.

It does not matter what religion you were raised in—or if you were raised in no religion at all. God loved the world—including the religious and the irreligious, the spiritual seekers and the militant atheists.

There is no one who falls outside the scope of "the world." And therefore there is no one who falls outside the scope of God's love.

THE INVITATION IS UNIVERSAL

Because God loved the world, the invitation to receive his love is extended to all. No one is excluded. No one is turned away. Jesus himself promised:

> *"All that the Father gives Me will come to Me, and the one who comes to Me I will certainly not cast out."* (John 6:37)
> *"Come to Me, all who are weary and heavy-laden, and I will give you rest."* (Matt 11:28)

The final invitation of the Bible echoes this universal welcome:

> *"The Spirit and the bride say, 'Come.' And let the one who hears say, 'Come.' And let the one who is thirsty come; let the one who wishes take the water of life without cost."* (Rev 22:17)

Let the one who wishes take the water of life without cost. This is the heart of John 3:16. God loved the world—the whole world—and anyone who wishes may come. The prophet Isaiah extended the same invitation centuries earlier:

> *"Ho! Every one who thirsts, come to the waters; and you who have no money come, buy and eat. Come, buy wine and milk without money and without cost."* (Isa 55:1)

"Every one who thirsts." Are you thirsty? Then the invitation is for you. "You who have no money." Do you come empty-handed?

Good—this cannot be bought. It is free. It is for the world. It is for you.

NO ONE WILL BE DISAPPOINTED

Perhaps you fear that if you come to God, you will be rejected. Perhaps you think your sins are too great, your past too dark, your record too shameful. Perhaps you believe that others are welcomed but you are not.

Scripture answers this fear directly:

> *"For the Scripture says, 'Whoever believes in Him will not be disappointed.'"* (Rom 10:11)

Whoever. That word is the practical application of "the world." Because God loved the world, *whoever* believes will be saved. Not *whoever is good enough.* Not *whoever has the right background.* Not *whoever has earned it.* Simply *whoever believes.*

And notice the promise: *will not be disappointed.* Not might not be. *Will not be.* This is a guarantee. If you come to Christ, you will not be turned away. If you believe in him, you will not be disappointed. God loved the world—and that includes you.

QUESTIONS FOR REFLECTION

- Have you ever felt that God's love might extend to others but not to you? What made you feel that way?
- How does it change your understanding of God to know that his plan has always been global—to bless all the families of the earth?
- What barriers or divisions in our world today need to hear the message that God loved "the world"—not just one group or nation?
- The invitation to come to Christ is extended to "whoever." What holds you back from responding?

- If God is "not wishing for any to perish but for all to come to repentance," what does that tell you about how he feels toward you right now?

A PRAYER

God, I am beginning to understand that your love is bigger than I imagined. You love the whole world—every nation, every tribe, every tongue, every people. And that means you love me. I have sometimes wondered if I was excluded, if your promises were for others but not for me. But your Word says "whoever," and that whoever includes me. Thank you that you do not show partiality. Thank you that there is no barrier I must overcome to come to you—you have broken down every wall. Help me to believe this more fully. Help me to come to you without fear, trusting that you will not cast me out.

Amen.

PART TWO

THE GIFT GOD GAVE

". . . that He gave His only begotten Son . . . "

—John 3:16b

4

" . . . That He Gave . . . "

Love in Action

"Thanks be to God for His indescribable gift!"

—2 CORINTHIANS 9:15

LOVE MUST ACT

"For God so loved the world, that He gave . . . "

We have spent three chapters exploring the God who loves. We have examined his character, his nature, and the scope of his affection. But now the verse takes a decisive turn. It moves from disposition to action, from feeling to deed, from sentiment to sacrifice. God did not merely *feel* love for the world—he *gave*.

The Greek word is *edōken* (ἔδωκεν)—"he gave." It is a simple word, but it transforms everything. Love that does not give is not love at all. Love that remains merely an emotion, a warm feeling, a private sentiment—that is not the love of God. Divine love acts. Divine love gives. Divine love costs something.[1]

1. The Greek word edōken (ἔδωκεν) is the aorist active indicative of didōmi, "to give." The aorist tense points to a definite historical act.

The apostle John, who recorded John 3:16, later wrote in one of his letters:

> *"Little children, let us not love with word or with tongue, but in deed and truth."* (1 John 3:18)

Not with word or tongue—but in *deed*. John understood what he had witnessed in Jesus Christ: love that acts, love that gives, love that does something. His fellow apostle James made the same point with a piercing illustration:

> *"If a brother or sister is without clothing and in need of daily food, and one of you says to them, 'Go in peace, be warmed and be filled,' and yet you do not give them what is necessary for their body, what use is that?"* (Jas 2:15–17)

What use is love that does not act? What good are warm words without warm clothing? What value is a sympathetic feeling without a substantive gift?

God's love is not useless. God's love is not mere sentiment. God loved—and therefore God *gave*.

THE GIVING GOD

Giving is not something God does occasionally. It is fundamental to who he is. Throughout Scripture, we see a God who gives—generously, lavishly, constantly.

In creation, God gave humanity everything needed for life. He gave plants for food. He gave Adam a partner. After the flood, he gave Noah permission to eat meat. To Abraham, he gave a promised land. To Moses, he gave the law—written by his own finger on tablets of stone. The psalmist declared that God's word is a gift: "Your word is a lamp to my feet and a light to my path."

God gives the ability to work and create wealth. He gives wisdom to those who ask. He gives strength to the weary and power to the weak. Every good thing we possess ultimately comes from him:

> *“Every good thing given and every perfect gift is from above, coming down from the Father of lights, with whom there is no variation or shifting shadow.”* (Jas 1:17)

Every good thing. *Every* perfect gift. The air you breathe, the food you eat, the relationships you enjoy, the abilities you possess—all are gifts from the giving God. Even those who do not acknowledge him receive his gifts:

> *“He did not leave Himself without witness, in that He did good and gave you rains from heaven and fruitful seasons, satisfying your hearts with food and gladness.”* (Acts 14:17)
>
> *“He causes His sun to rise on the evil and the good, and sends rain on the righteous and the unrighteous.”* (Matt 5:45)

This is remarkable. God gives even to those who reject him. He sends rain on the unrighteous. He satisfies the hearts of those who never thank him. He is a giver by nature, and he cannot stop giving.

But here is what makes John 3:16 so extraordinary: all of God’s previous gifts pale in comparison to this one. He does not merely give things—he gives *himself.* He does not merely give blessings—he gives his *Son.*

THE INDESCRIBABLE GIFT

Paul, overwhelmed by the generosity of God, exclaimed: “Thanks be to God for His indescribable gift!” The word “indescribable” is significant. It means that human language cannot adequately capture this gift. Words fail. Descriptions fall short. The gift of God’s Son is beyond what any language can express.

Consider what this gift includes. God did not give us an angel. He did not send a prophet. He did not dispatch a representative. He gave *his Son*—the second person of the Trinity, the eternal Word, the exact representation of his being. The prophet Isaiah, looking forward to this gift, wrote:

> *“For a child will be born to us, a son will be given to us.”* (Isa 9:6)

"A son will be *given* to us." The Son of God, given. The eternal One, delivered into human hands. The Lord of glory, handed over for sinners.

And with the Son, everything else is included. Paul reasoned this way:

> *"He who did not spare His own Son, but delivered Him over for us all, how will He not also with Him freely give us all things?"* (Rom 8:32)

The logic is irrefutable. If God gave his most precious possession—his own Son—will he withhold anything else? If he paid the ultimate price, will he now be stingy with lesser blessings? Of course not. The gift of the Son guarantees every other gift we will ever need.

WHAT JESUS GIVES

Throughout his ministry, Jesus described himself as one who gives. Consider the gifts he offers:

> *"If you knew the gift of God, and who it is who says to you, 'Give Me a drink,' you would have asked Him, and He would have given you living water."* (John 4:10)

Living water. Water that satisfies the deepest thirst of the human soul.

> *"For the bread of God is that which comes down out of heaven, and gives life to the world . . . I am the bread of life."* (John 6:33, 35)

The bread of life. Nourishment for the spiritually starving.

> *"I give eternal life to them, and they will never perish; and no one will snatch them out of My hand."* (John 10:28)

Eternal life. Life that never ends, life that cannot be taken away.

> *"Peace I leave with you; My peace I give to you; not as the world gives do I give to you. Do not let your heart be troubled, nor let it be fearful."* (John 14:27)

Peace. Not the fragile peace the world offers, but a peace that overcomes trouble and fear.

> *"If you then, being evil, know how to give good gifts to your children, how much more will your heavenly Father give the Holy Spirit to those who ask Him?"* (Luke 11:13)

The Holy Spirit. God himself, dwelling within his people.

Living water. The bread of life. Eternal life. Peace. The Holy Spirit. These are the gifts that come with the gift of the Son. And they are all free for the asking.

THE COSTLINESS OF THE GIFT

A gift is free to the one who receives it, but that does not mean it costs nothing. Someone must pay. And the gift of God's Son was purchased at an unimaginable price.

Consider the story of Abraham and Isaac in Genesis 22. God commanded Abraham: "Take now your son, your only son, whom you love, Isaac, and go to the land of Moriah, and offer him there as a burnt offering." The language is striking—"your son, your only son, whom you love." It echoes the language of John 3:16: "his only begotten Son."

Abraham obeyed. He took Isaac to Mount Moriah. He bound him on the altar. He raised the knife. And at the last moment, God intervened: "Do not stretch out your hand against the lad . . . for now I know that you fear God, since you have not withheld your son, your only son, from Me."

Abraham did not have to sacrifice his son. God provided a substitute—a ram caught in a thicket. But the story points forward to a day when there would be no substitute, no last-minute rescue, no intervention. On that day, God would not withhold his Son. He would give him completely, even to death on a cross.

John the Baptist, when he saw Jesus approaching, declared: "Behold, the Lamb of God who takes away the sin of the world!" A lamb for sacrifice. A lamb to be slain. This is the gift God gave—not a lamb from his flock, but the Lamb from his own heart, his only Son.

The prophet Isaiah described it centuries before it happened:

> *"All of us like sheep have gone astray, each of us has turned to his own way; but the LORD has caused the iniquity of us all to fall on Him."* (Isa 53:6)
>
> *"But the LORD was pleased to crush Him, putting Him to grief; if He would render Himself as a guilt offering . . . "* (Isa 53:10)

"The LORD was pleased to crush Him." These are among the most astonishing words in all of Scripture. The Father was pleased to crush the Son? How can this be? It was not that the Father delighted in the suffering itself, but that he delighted in what the suffering would accomplish—the salvation of sinners, the satisfaction of justice, the reconciliation of the world.

The gift cost the Father his Son. The gift cost the Son his life. This is no cheap grace, no easy salvation, no bargain-bin redemption. This is the most expensive gift ever given.

THE SON WHO WAS WILLING

It is important to understand that the Son was not an unwilling victim. He was not coerced or forced. He gave himself willingly, joyfully, lovingly. The Father's giving and the Son's self-giving are two sides of the same act of love.

> *"Although He existed in the form of God, [He] did not regard equality with God a thing to be grasped, but emptied Himself, taking the form of a bond-servant, and being made in the likeness of men. Being found in appearance as a man, He humbled Himself by becoming obedient to the point of death, even death on a cross."* (Phil 2:6–8)

He *emptied himself*. He *humbled himself*. He *became obedient*. These are active verbs. The Son chose to lay aside his glory. The Son chose to take on human flesh. The Son chose to submit to death—even the shameful, excruciating death of crucifixion.

> *"But when the fullness of the time came, God sent forth His Son, born of a woman, born under the Law, so that He might redeem those who were under the Law, that we might receive the adoption as sons."* (Gal 4:4–5)

God sent. The Son came. The Father's giving and the Son's coming are perfectly harmonized. And the purpose is clear: redemption and adoption. The Son came to buy us back from slavery and to bring us into the family of God.

> *"For you know the grace of our Lord Jesus Christ, that though He was rich, yet for your sake He became poor, so that you through His poverty might become rich."* (2 Cor 8:9)

Though he was rich—possessing all the glory of heaven—he became poor, taking on the poverty of human existence, so that we who are spiritually bankrupt might become rich in him. This is the great exchange at the heart of the gospel: his poverty for our riches, his death for our life, his condemnation for our justification.

GRACE: THE NATURE OF THE GIFT

The Bible has a word for this kind of giving. The word is *grace*.

In Greek, the word is *charis* (χάρις). It refers to a gift that is freely given, unearned, undeserved. Grace is the opposite of wages. Wages are earned; grace is given. Wages are owed; grace is freely bestowed. Wages are a matter of debt; grace is a matter of generosity.

> *"For by grace you have been saved through faith; and that not of yourselves, it is the gift of God; not as a result of works, so that no one may boast."* (Eph 2:8–9)

Notice the key words: *grace, gift, not of yourselves, not as a result of works*. Salvation is a gift. It cannot be earned. It cannot be achieved. It can only be received.

> *"For the wages of sin is death, but the free gift of God is eternal life in Christ Jesus our Lord."* (Rom 6:23)

Here is the contrast laid bare. Wages—what we have earned—is death. We have worked hard for our condemnation; we have earned it by our sins. But eternal life is not a wage; it is a *free gift*. We did not earn it. We cannot earn it. God simply gives it to those who receive it in Christ.

WHY GRACE MUST BE FREE

The New Testament is emphatic: grace and works cannot be mixed. If salvation is by grace, it cannot be by works. If it is by works, it is no longer grace.

> *"But if it is by grace, it is no longer on the basis of works, otherwise grace is no longer grace."* (Rom 11:6)
>
> *"Now to the one who works, his wage is not credited as a favor, but as what is due. But to the one who does not work, but believes in Him who justifies the ungodly, his faith is credited as righteousness."* (Rom 4:4–5)

This is the heart of the gospel: God "justifies the ungodly." He does not justify those who have made themselves godly. He does not reward those who have earned it. He freely gives righteousness to those who have no righteousness of their own—to those who simply believe.

Why must grace be free? Because we could never earn it. Our best efforts are pathetically inadequate:

> *"He saved us, not on the basis of deeds which we have done in righteousness, but according to His mercy."* (Titus 3:5)
> *"But if righteousness comes through the Law, then Christ died needlessly."* (Gal 2:21)

If we could have saved ourselves by our own efforts, Christ's death was unnecessary. The very fact that God gave his Son proves that no other solution was possible. We needed a gift because we could never earn salvation.

THE IMPOSSIBILITY OF SELF-SALVATION

Perhaps you are troubled by this. Perhaps you have been taught that you need to earn your way to God—that if you are good enough, religious enough, moral enough, you will be accepted. The Bible shatters this illusion.

> *"For all of us have become like one who is unclean, and all our righteous deeds are like a filthy garment."* (Isa 64:6)

Our *righteous* deeds—our best efforts, our most impressive achievements—are like filthy rags in God's sight. If our righteousness is filthy, what hope do we have of impressing a holy God? None. Absolutely none.

> *"Because by the works of the Law no flesh will be justified in His sight."* (Rom 3:20)
>
> *"For as many as are of the works of the Law are under a curse; for it is written, 'Cursed is everyone who does not abide by all things written in the book of the law, to perform them.'"* (Gal 3:10)

The law does not save us; it condemns us. It shows us how far we fall short. It demands perfect obedience—and we have not given it. We have not kept all things written in the law. Therefore, trying to be saved by our own works puts us under a curse, not a blessing.

This is why salvation must be a gift. We cannot buy it, earn it, achieve it, or deserve it. We can only receive it.

TWO MEN IN THE TEMPLE

Jesus told a parable that perfectly illustrates the difference between those who try to earn God's favor and those who receive it as a gift.

Two men went to the temple to pray. One was a Pharisee—a religious leader known for strict obedience to the law. The other was a tax collector—a class of people despised for their corruption and collaboration with the Roman occupiers.

The Pharisee stood and prayed: "God, I thank You that I am not like other people: swindlers, unjust, adulterers, or even like this tax collector. I fast twice a week; I pay tithes of all that I get." His prayer was a resume. He listed his accomplishments, his moral superiority, his religious achievements. He came to God with his hands full of good works.

The tax collector stood at a distance. He would not even lift his eyes to heaven. He beat his breast in anguish and prayed: "God, be merciful to me, the sinner!" That was all. No resume. No list of achievements. Just a plea for mercy. He came to God with empty hands.

Jesus concluded: "I tell you, this man went to his house justified rather than the other; for everyone who exalts himself will be humbled, but he who humbles himself will be exalted."

The tax collector went home justified—declared righteous before God. Why? Not because of what he had done, but because of what he received. He asked for mercy, and God gave it. He asked for grace, and God poured it out. He came empty-handed, and God filled his hands with the gift of forgiveness.

Which man are you? Are you coming to God with your hands full of achievements, hoping to impress him with your goodness? Or are you coming empty-handed, ready to receive what only grace can give?

THE GIFT IS OFFERED TO YOU

God gave his Son. That is an accomplished fact—a gift already given. But a gift is not yours until you receive it. A present under the tree remains wrapped until someone opens it. An inheritance sits unclaimed until the heir accepts it.

The gift of salvation is offered to you today. It has already been purchased. The price has already been paid. The Son has already been given. Now the gift is extended, waiting for you to receive it.

> *"The Spirit and the bride say, 'Come.' And let the one who hears say, 'Come.' And let the one who is thirsty come; let the one who wishes take the water of life without cost."* (Rev 22:17)

Without cost. Free. A gift. You do not have to pay for it. You do not have to earn it. You simply have to *come* and *take.*

> *"Ho! Every one who thirsts, come to the waters; and you who have no money come, buy and eat. Come, buy wine and milk without money and without cost."* (Isa 55:1)

"You who have no money"—you who have nothing to offer. Come. Buy without money. Receive without cost. This is grace. This is the nature of the gift.

> *"If anyone is thirsty, let him come to Me and drink. He who believes in Me, as the Scripture said, 'From his innermost being will flow rivers of living water.'"* (John 7:37–38)

"If anyone is thirsty"—the invitation is open. "Let him come to Me"—the direction is clear. "And drink"—the action is simple. Are you thirsty? Then come. Drink. Receive the gift.

QUESTIONS FOR REFLECTION

- What is the difference between love as a feeling and love as an action? Why is it significant that God "gave" rather than merely "felt"?
- Have you ever tried to earn God's favor through your own efforts? What did this chapter reveal about why that approach cannot work?
- In the parable of the Pharisee and the tax collector, which man do you most identify with? Why?
- What does it mean to you that salvation is described as a "gift"? How does this change the way you think about your relationship with God?
- The invitation is to come "without cost." What is preventing you from receiving God's gift today?

A PRAYER

God, I am beginning to understand that your love is not just a feeling—it is an action. You did not merely feel affection for me from a distance; you gave. You gave your Son. You gave the most precious thing in the universe for someone like me. I confess that I have often tried to earn your favor, to impress you with my goodness, to pay my own way. But I see now that this is impossible. My righteousness is filthy rags. My best efforts fall short. I need grace. I need a gift. So I come to you today with empty hands. I do not come with achievements or accomplishments. I come as the tax collector: 'God, be merciful to me, the sinner!' Thank you that you give to those who have nothing to offer. Thank you that the water of life is without cost. Help me to receive what I could never earn.

Amen.

5

"... His Only Begotten Son ..."

The Identity of the Gift

"And the Word became flesh, and dwelt among us, and we saw His glory, glory as of the only begotten from the Father, full of grace and truth."

—John 1:14

THE MOST IMPORTANT QUESTION

"For God so loved the world, that He gave His only begotten Son ..."

We have seen that God loved. We have seen that God gave. Now we must examine *what*—or more precisely, *whom*—God gave. The answer to this question is the most important claim in all of Christianity. Everything hinges on it.

God gave "His only begotten Son." Three words packed with meaning: *His*—belonging to God, from God's own being. *Only begotten*—unique, one of a kind, in a category all his own. *Son*—sharing the nature of the Father, bearing the family likeness, possessing the divine essence.

Who is this Son? What does it mean that he is "only begotten"? And why does it matter? The answers to these questions will reveal the heart of the Christian faith.

WHAT DOES "ONLY BEGOTTEN" MEAN?

The phrase "only begotten" translates the Greek word *monogenēs* (μονογενής). This word has sometimes been misunderstood to mean "only born" or "only created," as if the Son had a beginning, as if there was a time when he did not exist. But this is not what the word means.[1]

Monogenēs is composed of two parts: *monos* ("only") and *genos* ("kind" or "type"). It does not refer to origin or birth but to *uniqueness*. The Son is the "one and only" Son—unique, in a class by himself, without peer or parallel.

John uses this word repeatedly to describe Jesus:

"The Word became flesh, and dwelt among us, and we saw His glory, glory as of the *only begotten* from the Father."

"No one has seen God at any time; the *only begotten* God who is in the bosom of the Father, He has explained Him."

"He who believes in Him is not judged; he who does not believe has been judged already, because he has not believed in the name of the *only begotten* Son of God."

"By this the love of God was manifested in us, that God has sent His *only begotten* Son into the world so that we might live through Him."

The emphasis in every case is on the unique, incomparable status of the Son. He is not one son among many. He is the *only* Son—the one and only of his kind.

We see this meaning clearly in Hebrews 11:17, where Isaac is called Abraham's *monogenēs*—his "only begotten" son. But Abraham had other sons! Ishmael was born before Isaac, and Abraham later had six sons through Keturah. So how could Isaac be called

1. The Greek word monogenēs (μονογενής) means "unique," "one of a kind," or "only." It does not imply origin or creation. See D. A. Carson, The Gospel According to John (Grand Rapids: Eerdmans, 1991).

his "only begotten"? Because Isaac was unique—the child of promise, the one through whom God's covenant would be fulfilled. He was in a category by himself.

In the same way, Jesus is God's *monogenēs*—not because there are no other "sons of God" in Scripture (believers are called sons of God), but because Jesus is unique. He alone is the eternal Son. He alone shares the Father's nature. He alone is God of God, Light of Light, true God of true God.

THE SON IS GOD

The most astonishing claim of the Christian faith is that this Son who was given is himself God. Not a god. Not godlike. Not a divine messenger or an exalted angel. *God*—in the fullest, most absolute sense of the word.

The Gospel of John begins with this declaration:

> *"In the beginning was the Word, and the Word was with God, and the Word was God."* (John 1:1)

Three claims in one verse. First: "In the beginning was the Word." The Word already *was*—he did not come into being at the beginning; he already existed when the beginning began. Second: "The Word was with God." The Word is distinct from the Father—a separate person in relationship with God. Third: "The Word was God." The Word shares the divine nature; he is himself God.

This Word, John tells us, is none other than Jesus Christ. And this Word was the agent of creation:

> *"All things came into being through Him, and apart from Him nothing came into being that has come into being."* (John 1:3)

All things. Nothing came into being apart from him. The Son is not a creature; he is the Creator. The apostle Paul affirms the same truth:

> *"For by Him all things were created, both in the heavens and on earth, visible and invisible, whether thrones or*

> *dominions or rulers or authorities—all things have been created through Him and for Him. He is before all things, and in Him all things hold together."* (Col 1:16)

The writer of Hebrews adds:

> *"In these last days [God] has spoken to us in His Son, whom He appointed heir of all things, through whom also He made the world. And He is the radiance of His glory and the exact representation of His nature, and upholds all things by the word of His power."* (Heb 1:2–3)

The Son is the "radiance of His glory"—the outshining of the Father's splendor. He is the "exact representation of His nature"—the perfect image, the precise imprint of the divine being. This is no mere creature. This is God himself.

JESUS CLAIMED TO BE GOD

The deity of Christ is not merely a doctrine invented by later Christians. Jesus himself made claims that only God could make.

When the Jews challenged him, Jesus responded: "Truly, truly, I say to you, before Abraham was born, I am." "I am"—not "I was." Jesus claimed eternal existence, using the present tense "I am" (*egō eimi*). This was the very name God revealed to Moses at the burning bush: "I AM WHO I AM." Jesus was claiming to be the eternal, self-existent God of Israel.

The Jews understood exactly what he was claiming. They picked up stones to kill him for blasphemy.

On another occasion, Jesus declared: "I and the Father are one." Again, the Jews picked up stones. When Jesus asked why, they answered: "For a good work we do not stone You, but for blasphemy; and because You, being a man, make Yourself out to be God." They understood his claim perfectly. Jesus was making himself equal with God.

After the resurrection, when Thomas saw the risen Jesus, he fell at his feet and exclaimed: "My Lord and my God!" Jesus did not correct him. He did not say, "Do not call me God—I'm only a prophet." He accepted the worship. He received the title. Because it was true.

THE TESTIMONY OF THE APOSTLES

The apostles who walked with Jesus and wrote the New Testament were unambiguous: Jesus Christ is God.

Paul wrote that Christ Jesus, "although He existed in the form of God, did not regard equality with God a thing to be grasped." He existed in the "form" (*morphē*) of God—not merely the appearance, but the essential nature. He possessed "equality with God."

Paul declared that "in Him all the fullness of Deity dwells in bodily form." Not some deity, not partial deity—"all the fullness of Deity." Everything that God is dwells in Christ.

Paul called Jesus "our great God and Savior." The writer of Hebrews says of the Son, "Your throne, O God, is forever and ever." Paul also wrote that Christ is "God blessed forever."

The testimony is consistent and overwhelming. The Son given in John 3:16 is not a mere man, not an angel, not a prophet. He is God himself, come in human flesh.

THE SON BECAME MAN

But the astonishing claim does not stop there. This Son who is God also became man. The eternal entered time. The infinite took on finite flesh. The Creator became a creature.

> *"And the Word became flesh, and dwelt among us."* (John 1:14)

The Word "became" (*egeneto*) flesh. This was a real becoming—not a disguise, not an appearance, not a temporary costume. The Son took on human nature permanently. He added humanity to his deity without losing or diminishing his divinity.

> *"[He] emptied Himself, taking the form of a bond-servant, and being made in the likeness of men. Being found in*

> *appearance as a man, He humbled Himself by becoming obedient to the point of death, even death on a cross."* (Phil 2:7–8)
>
> *"But when the fullness of the time came, God sent forth His Son, born of a woman, born under the Law."* (Gal 4:4)

"Born of a woman." The Son entered the world the way every human enters—through a mother's womb. He was nursed, he was weaned, he learned to walk and talk. He grew in wisdom and stature. He knew childhood and adolescence and adulthood. He was truly, fully, completely human.

> *"Therefore, since the children share in flesh and blood, He Himself likewise also partook of the same, that through death He might render powerless him who had the power of death, that is, the devil."* (Heb 2:14)

He "partook" of flesh and blood. He shared in our humanity. He experienced what we experience. He was not a phantom or an illusion but a real human being with a real human body, a real human mind, real human emotions.

WHY THE INCARNATION MATTERS

Why did the Son have to become human? Why could not God simply forgive from heaven? Why this strange union of divine and human in one person?

The answer lies in what salvation required. Salvation is not merely forgiveness—it is redemption, rescue, reconciliation. And for this, the Savior had to be both God and man.

He Had to Be Human to Represent Us

> *"Therefore, He had to be made like His brethren in all things, so that He might become a merciful and faithful high priest in things pertaining to God, to make propitiation for the sins of the people."* (Heb 2:17)

He "had to be made like His brethren." Humanity sinned; humanity must pay the penalty. But no mere human could bear the infinite weight of sin against an infinite God. So the Son became human—not to replace us but to *represent* us. He stood in our place. He took what we deserved. He died the death we earned.

He Had to Be Human to Sympathize with Us

> *"For we do not have a high priest who cannot sympathize with our weaknesses, but One who has been tempted in all things as we are, yet without sin."* (Heb 4:15)

Jesus knows what it is to be human. He knows hunger—he fasted forty days in the wilderness. He knows weariness—he sat down at the well, exhausted from his journey. He knows grief—he wept at the tomb of his friend Lazarus. He knows anguish—his soul was "deeply grieved, to the point of death" in Gethsemane.

When you come to Jesus, you do not come to someone who cannot understand. You come to one who has walked where you walk, felt what you feel, faced what you face. He knows. He sympathizes. He understands.

He Had to Be God to Save Us

But being human alone was not enough. To bear the infinite weight of sin required an infinite person. Only God could absorb the full penalty of divine wrath. Only God could satisfy the demands of divine justice. Only God could accomplish what needed to be done.

> *"For there is one God, and one mediator also between God and men, the man Christ Jesus."* (1 Tim 2:5)

One mediator. One who stands between God and humanity, with a foot in each world. He is the "man Christ Jesus"—truly human. But he is also the one who bridges the gap to God—because he *is* God. No mere creature could accomplish this. Only the God-man could reconcile God and humanity.

This is why the church has always confessed that Jesus Christ is truly God and truly man—two natures united in one person, without confusion, without change, without division, without separation. Remove either nature and salvation collapses. A Jesus who is only man cannot save us. A Jesus who is only God cannot represent us. But the Jesus of John 3:16—God's only begotten Son—is both. And therefore he can do what needed to be done.

WHY ONLY JESUS?

In a world of many religions, many spiritual teachers, many paths claiming to lead to God—why Jesus? Why is he the gift that God gave? Why not Buddha, Muhammad, Krishna, or any of the other religious figures history has produced?

The answer flows from everything we have seen. Salvation requires a Savior who is both human and divine. No other religious figure makes this claim or meets this requirement.

Only Jesus Was Sinless

> *"For it was fitting for us to have such a high priest, holy, innocent, undefiled, separated from sinners and exalted above the heavens; who does not need daily, like those high priests, to offer up sacrifices, first for His own sins and then for the sins of the people, because this He did once for all when He offered up Himself."* (Heb 7:26–27)

Jesus was "holy, innocent, undefiled." He did not need to offer sacrifice for his own sins because he had none. Every other human being—including every religious founder—is a sinner in need of salvation. They cannot save others because they cannot even save themselves. Only Jesus was qualified to be the perfect sacrifice.

> *"You were not redeemed with perishable things like silver or gold from your futile way of life inherited from your forefathers, but with precious blood, as of a lamb unblemished and spotless, the blood of Christ."* (1 Pet 1:18–19)

"He made Him who knew no sin to be sin on our behalf, so that we might become the righteousness of God in Him." (2 Cor 5:21)

"He who knew no sin." This is the unique qualification of Jesus Christ. He alone was sinless. He alone could be the unblemished lamb. He alone could take our sin upon himself because he had no sin of his own.

Only Jesus Died for Sin

Buddha did not die for sin—he died of food poisoning. Muhammad did not die for sin—he died of fever. No other religious figure claimed to die as a sacrifice for the sins of the world. Only Jesus.

"And according to the Law, one may almost say, all things are cleansed with blood, and without shedding of blood there is no forgiveness." (Heb 9:22)

"Without shedding of blood there is no forgiveness." This is the divine requirement. Sin must be paid for. Justice must be satisfied. And the only currency sufficient is the blood of the sinless Son of God.

"For it is impossible for the blood of bulls and goats to take away sins." (Heb 10:4)

Animal sacrifices could never truly take away sin—they were shadows, pointers, anticipations of the true sacrifice to come. Only the blood of Christ, the God-man, could accomplish what all other sacrifices could only symbolize.

Only Jesus Rose from the Dead

Buddha is dead. Muhammad is dead. Every other religious founder is dead and remains dead. Only Jesus conquered death. Only Jesus walked out of the tomb. Only Jesus is alive today.

The resurrection is the Father's vindication of the Son, the proof that his sacrifice was accepted, the guarantee that his victory over sin and death is complete. A dead savior cannot save. But Jesus is not dead. He is alive, and because he lives, those who believe in him will live also.

The medieval theologian Anselm put it this way: only a human being ought to make satisfaction for human sin, but only God could make sufficient satisfaction. Therefore, the Savior must be both God and man. And there is only one such person in all of history: Jesus Christ, the only begotten Son of God.

JESUS'S EXCLUSIVE CLAIMS

Jesus himself made claims that no other religious figure has made:

> *"I am the way, and the truth, and the life; no one comes to the Father but through Me."* (John 14:6)

Not *a* way—*the* way. Not *a* truth—*the* truth. Not *a* life—*the* life. And then the exclusive claim: "No one comes to the Father but through Me." There is no other path. There is no alternative route. Jesus is the only way to God.

His apostles echoed this exclusivity:

> *"And there is salvation in no one else; for there is no other name under heaven that has been given among men by which we must be saved."* (Acts 4:12)
>
> *"For there is one God, and one mediator also between God and men, the man Christ Jesus, who gave Himself as a ransom for all."* (1 Tim 2:5–6)

"No other name." "One mediator." The Christian claim is unapologetically exclusive. Not because Christians are arrogant, but because the nature of salvation demands it. If only the God-man can save, and if Jesus is the only God-man, then Jesus is the only Savior.

LORD, LIAR, OR LUNATIC?

The claims of Jesus force a decision. C. S. Lewis famously articulated the logic:[2]

A man who claimed the things Jesus claimed must be one of three things. Either he was a liar—he knew his claims were false and deceived millions deliberately. Or he was a lunatic—he genuinely believed he was God but was tragically deluded. Or he was who he claimed to be—Lord.

There is no fourth option. You cannot say, "Jesus was a great moral teacher, but he was not God." A merely human Jesus who claimed to be God would be neither great nor moral—he would be either wicked or insane. The only way to honor Jesus as a good teacher is to accept his teaching about himself: that he is the only begotten Son of God.

Jesus did not leave the door open for people to admire him as merely a wise sage. He claimed the authority to forgive sins—something only God can do. He claimed that the Father "has given all judgment to the Son, so that all will honor the Son even as they honor the Father." He claimed that "all authority has been given to Me in heaven and on earth." He commanded his followers to baptize in his name alongside the Father and the Spirit. He received worship—and worship belongs to God alone.

The evidence points to one conclusion: Jesus is who he claimed to be. He is the only begotten Son of God. He is the gift the Father gave. He is the only hope for sinners like you and me.

DO YOU KNOW HIM?

The purpose of John 3:16 is not merely to inform you about God's Son but to invite you to know him. Jesus said to the religious scholars of his day:

> *"You search the Scriptures because you think that in them you have eternal life; it is these that testify about Me; and*

2. C. S. Lewis, Mere Christianity (New York: HarperOne, 2001), 52–53. Originally published 1952.

> *you are unwilling to come to Me so that you may have life."*
> (John 5:39–40)

Knowledge about Jesus is not the same as knowing Jesus. You can study theology, memorize Scripture, and understand doctrine—and still miss the whole point. The Scriptures testify about him. They point to him. They lead to him. But at some point, you must come to *him*.

The Son of God became the Son of Man so that the sons of men could become sons of God. He who knew no sin became sin for us. He who was rich became poor so that we through his poverty might become rich. He who was life itself died so that those who were dead might live.

This is the gift. This is the one who was given. This is the only begotten Son of God. Do you know him? Have you come to him? Have you received the gift?

Paul wrote that the Son "is the image of the invisible God." Hebrews says he is "the exact representation of His nature." Jesus told Philip, "He who has seen Me has seen the Father." If you want to know what God is like, look at Jesus. If you want to understand God's heart, see it displayed in the Son. If you want to experience God's love, receive it through the only begotten.

QUESTIONS FOR REFLECTION

- Before reading this chapter, what did you believe about Jesus? Was he merely a good teacher, a prophet, or something more?
- Why is it significant that Jesus is "only begotten"—unique, one of a kind? What does this mean for how we should respond to him?
- How does Jesus being both fully God and fully human make salvation possible? Why could not a mere human or a mere angel accomplish what Jesus accomplished?
- Jesus claimed to be "the way, the truth, and the life"—the only way to the Father. How do you respond to this exclusive claim?

- C. S. Lewis said Jesus must be Lord, liar, or lunatic. Which do you believe he is, and why?

A PRAYER

Lord Jesus, I am beginning to understand who you truly are. You are not merely a teacher or a prophet—you are the only begotten Son of God. You are God in human flesh. You existed before the world began. You created all things. You left the glory of heaven and took on the poverty of human existence—for me. You who knew no sin became sin for me. You who are life itself died for me. I confess that I have not always honored you as you deserve. I have treated you as less than you are. But I want to know you—not just know about you, but truly know you. Open my eyes to see your glory. Open my heart to receive your gift. Show me the Father, for you have said that whoever has seen you has seen the Father. I come to you today because there is no other way, no other truth, no other life. You alone are the Savior. Be my Savior.

Amen.

6

The Cross

What the Gift Cost

"He made Him who knew no sin to be sin on our behalf, so that we might become the righteousness of God in Him."

—2 CORINTHIANS 5:21

THE DARKEST DAY IN HISTORY

We have been tracing the words of John 3:16: "For God so loved the world, that He gave His only begotten Son." We have examined the God who loves, the nature of that love, the world that is loved, the act of giving, and the identity of the gift—the only begotten Son of God.

But to understand what it means that God "gave" his Son, we must go to a specific place on a specific day. We must go to a hill outside Jerusalem, to a Friday afternoon around AD 33, to an instrument of execution so brutal that civilized people did not speak of it in polite company.

We must go to the cross.

The cross is not an afterthought in God's plan. It is not a tragic accident that God somehow turned to good. The cross is the very center of human history, the hinge on which everything turns, the moment toward which all of Scripture points and from which all of salvation flows. When John 3:16 says God "gave" his Son, this is what it means: God gave him to die. God gave him to the cross.

THE HISTORICAL REALITY

Before we explore the meaning of the cross, we must establish its reality. The crucifixion of Jesus of Nazareth is one of the best-attested facts of ancient history. It is confirmed not only by the four Gospels but also by secular historians who had no interest in promoting Christianity.

The Roman historian Tacitus, writing around AD 116, recorded that "Christus" was executed under Pontius Pilate during the reign of Tiberius. The Jewish historian Josephus, writing in the late first century, also mentioned Jesus's death under Pilate. Even the Babylonian Talmud, a Jewish source hostile to Christianity, confirms that Jesus was executed on the eve of Passover.

No serious historian doubts that Jesus of Nazareth was crucified under Pontius Pilate. The question is not whether it happened, but what it means.

THE HORROR OF CRUCIFIXION

We have become so familiar with the cross that we have forgotten how horrible it was. We wear crosses as jewelry, hang them on our walls, place them atop our churches. We have sanitized and sentimentalized the most brutal form of execution ever devised.

Crucifixion was designed not simply to kill but to torture, to humiliate, to terrorize. The Roman statesman Cicero called it "the cruelest and most hideous punishment." It was reserved for slaves, pirates, and enemies of the state—never for Roman citizens. To die on a cross was to die the death of the lowest, the most despised, the most cursed.[1]

1. Cicero, Against Verres 2.5.165: "crudelissimum taeterrimumque

For Jews, crucifixion carried an additional horror. The law of Moses declared: "Cursed is everyone who hangs on a tree." To be crucified was to be under God's curse. This is why Paul wrote that the message of Christ crucified was "a stumbling block to Jews." How could the Messiah, God's chosen one, die the death of the cursed?

Before the crucifixion, Jesus was flogged—beaten with a whip embedded with bone and metal that tore the flesh from his back. He was mocked, spat upon, crowned with thorns. Isaiah's prophecy was fulfilled: "His appearance was marred more than any man."

Then he was led to Golgotha—"the place of the skull"—and nailed to the cross. There he hung between two criminals, naked, exposed, struggling for breath, as his life slowly drained away.

At noon, darkness fell over the land—darkness that lasted three hours, as if creation itself could not bear to watch. And from the darkness came a cry that still echoes through history: "My God, My God, why have You forsaken Me?"

This is the gift. This is what it cost. This is what God "gave."

THE MEANING OF THE CROSS: SUBSTITUTION

But why? Why did the Son of God have to die this way? What was accomplished on that cross?

The Bible answers with a word that has fallen out of favor in our age but remains at the heart of the gospel: *substitution.* Jesus died *in our place.* He took what we deserved so that we could receive what he deserved.

> *"For even the Son of Man did not come to be served, but to serve, and to give His life a ransom for many."* (Mark 10:45)

A "ransom" is a price paid to secure someone's release. Jesus gave his life as the ransom price—"for" (Greek *anti*, meaning "in the place of") many. His death was substitutionary. He died so that others would not have to die.

supplicium" ("the cruelest and most hideous punishment").

> *"For Christ also died for sins once for all, the just for the unjust, so that He might bring us to God."* (1 Pet 3:18)

"The just for the unjust." The innocent for the guilty. The righteous for the unrighteous. This is the great exchange at the heart of the gospel.

> *"He made Him who knew no sin to be sin on our behalf, so that we might become the righteousness of God in Him."* (2 Cor 5:21)

God made Jesus "to be sin." Not that Jesus became sinful—he remained morally perfect. But God treated him as if he were sin itself. All our guilt, all our rebellion, all our failure was placed upon him. And in exchange, his righteousness is given to us.

> *"Christ redeemed us from the curse of the Law, having become a curse for us—for it is written, 'Cursed is everyone who hangs on a tree.'"* (Gal 3:13)

He "became a curse for us." The curse that should have fallen on us fell on him. The judgment we deserved was poured out on him. This is what Isaiah saw seven hundred years before it happened:

> *"But He was pierced through for our transgressions, He was crushed for our iniquities; the chastening for our well-being fell upon Him, and by His scourging we are healed. All of us like sheep have gone astray, each of us has turned to his own way; but the LORD has caused the iniquity of us all to fall on Him."* (Isa 53:5–6)

"Pierced through for *our* transgressions." "Crushed for *our* iniquities." "The iniquity of us *all* fell on *Him*." The language is unmistakable. He suffered what we should have suffered. He bore what we should have borne. He was our substitute.

THE MEANING OF THE CROSS: PROPITIATION

Another word the Bible uses to describe what happened on the cross is *propitiation*. This is an unfamiliar word to most modern readers, but it captures something essential.

Propitiation means the turning away of wrath. It is a sacrifice that satisfies the demands of a holy God, that absorbs his righteous anger, that makes it possible for him to be favorable toward those who were once his enemies.

> *"God displayed [Christ Jesus] publicly as a propitiation in His blood through faith. This was to demonstrate His righteousness, because in the forbearance of God He passed over the sins previously committed; for the demonstration, I say, of His righteousness at the present time, so that He would be just and the justifier of the one who has faith in Jesus."* (Rom 3:25–26)

Notice the purpose: so that God could be both "just and the justifier." This is the heart of the matter. God is just—he cannot simply overlook sin. But God also wants to justify sinners—to declare them righteous, to welcome them into his family. How can he do both? Through the propitiation accomplished by Christ.

> *"He Himself is the propitiation for our sins; and not for ours only, but also for those of the whole world."* (1 John 2:2)
>
> *"In this is love, not that we loved God, but that He loved us and sent His Son to be the propitiation for our sins."* (1 John 4:10)

Some people are uncomfortable with the idea of God's wrath. They prefer to think of God as only loving, never angry. But this sentimentality does not take sin seriously. If God were not angry at evil, he would not be good. A God who looks at injustice, cruelty, and wickedness and feels nothing would be a moral monster.

> *"Much more then, having now been justified by His blood, we shall be saved from the wrath of God through Him."* (Rom 5:9)

"The wrath of God" is real. It is his settled opposition to all that is evil, his holy hatred of sin. And apart from Christ, it rests on every sinner. But through the cross, that wrath has been satisfied. The propitiation has been made. Those who are in Christ are safe from wrath forever.

THE MEANING OF THE CROSS: REDEMPTION

A third word the Bible uses for what Christ accomplished is *redemption.* To redeem means to buy back, to purchase someone's freedom. It is the language of the slave market.

> *"You were not redeemed with perishable things like silver or gold from your futile way of life inherited from your forefathers, but with precious blood, as of a lamb unblemished and spotless, the blood of Christ."* (1 Pet 1:18–19)

We were slaves—slaves to sin, slaves to fear, slaves to futile ways of living. And we could not free ourselves. But Christ paid the price. Not with silver or gold, but with something infinitely more valuable: his own blood.

> *"In Him we have redemption through His blood, the forgiveness of our trespasses, according to the riches of His grace."* (Eph 1:7)
>
> *"For He rescued us from the domain of darkness, and transferred us to the kingdom of His beloved Son, in whom we have redemption, the forgiveness of sins."* (Col 1:13–14)
>
> *"[He] gave Himself for us to redeem us from every lawless deed, and to purify for Himself a people for His own possession, zealous for good deeds."* (Titus 2:14)

In heaven, the redeemed sing this song:

> *"Worthy are You to take the book and to break its seals; for You were slain, and purchased for God with Your blood men from every tribe and tongue and people and nation."* (Rev 5:9)

"You were slain, and purchased for God with Your blood." This is redemption. We have been bought. We belong to him. We are no longer slaves to sin but servants of the living God—and that servanthood is perfect freedom.

WHY THE CROSS WAS NECESSARY

But why was all of this necessary? Could not God simply have forgiven sins without the cross? Could not an all-powerful God have found another way?

The answer lies in the nature of God himself—specifically, in the collision between his love and his justice.

God's Justice Demands Punishment

God is just. He cannot simply overlook sin as if it does not matter. Sin is not a minor issue—it is rebellion against the infinite, holy Creator of the universe. It carries an infinite penalty.

"For all have sinned and fall short of the glory of God." This is the human condition. We have all missed the mark. We have all fallen short. And the penalty is severe: "For the wages of sin is death." "The soul who sins will die."

God's holiness cannot tolerate sin. His "eyes are too pure to approve evil." He cannot have fellowship with wickedness. And his justice requires that sin be punished: "He will by no means leave the guilty unpunished."

If God simply ignored sin, he would not be just. He would be complicit with evil. His throne is founded on righteousness and justice—and a foundation cannot be compromised without the whole structure collapsing.

God's Love Desires Salvation

But God is also love. And love does not want to destroy—it wants to save. God takes no pleasure in the death of the wicked. He desires that all would come to repentance. His heart yearns for reconciliation.

Here is the dilemma: How can God be true to his justice (which demands punishment) and true to his love (which desires salvation)? How can he remain just and yet justify sinners? How can he punish sin and yet forgive sinners?

The Cross Solves the Dilemma

The cross is the answer. At the cross, God's justice and God's love meet. Sin is punished—but not in the sinner. The penalty is paid—but by a substitute. Justice is satisfied—and mercy is extended.

As John Stott wrote, "The concept of substitution may be said to lie at the heart of both sin and salvation. For the essence of sin is man substituting himself for God, while the essence of salvation is God substituting himself for man."[2]

God did not compromise his justice. Every sin has been punished. God did not abandon his love. Every sinner can be saved. The cross made it possible for God to be "just and the justifier of the one who has faith in Jesus."

This is why the cross was necessary. Not because God lacked power to save in some other way, but because his own character—his justice and his love together—required it. The cross is not arbitrary; it is the only solution that honors both who God is and what we need.

THE SEVEN LAST WORDS

From the cross, Jesus spoke seven times. These "seven last words" reveal the heart of what was happening in those dark hours.

"Father, forgive them; for they do not know what they are doing." Even as they drove nails through his hands, Jesus prayed for his executioners. The first word from the cross is a word of forgiveness.

"Truly I say to you, today you shall be with Me in Paradise." To a criminal dying beside him—a man with no time for good works, no opportunity for religious rituals—Jesus promised immediate entrance into Paradise. The second word is a word of salvation.

"Woman, behold, your son . . . Behold, your mother." Even in his agony, Jesus cared for his mother, entrusting her to the beloved disciple. The third word is a word of compassion.

2. John R. W. Stott, The Cross of Christ (Downers Grove: IVP, 1986), 160.

"My God, My God, why have You forsaken Me?" This is the cry of dereliction—the moment when Jesus experienced the full weight of divine abandonment. He who had been eternally one with the Father was now separated by the sin he bore. The fourth word is a word of desolation.

"I am thirsty." The one who offered living water now thirsted. The Creator of all things needed a drink. The fifth word is a word of humanity.

"It is finished." This is not a cry of defeat but a shout of triumph. The work is complete. The price is paid. The mission is accomplished. The sixth word is a word of victory.

"Father, into Your hands I commit My spirit." With these words, Jesus voluntarily gave up his life. No one took it from him; he laid it down of his own accord. The seventh word is a word of trust.

"IT IS FINISHED"

Of all the words from the cross, none is more important than the sixth: "It is finished."

In Greek, this is one word: *tetelestai* (τετέλεσται). It means "completed," "accomplished," "fulfilled." It is a word of finality. Nothing more needs to be done. Nothing more *can* be done. The work is finished.

Archaeologists have discovered ancient receipts with this word written across them—*tetelestai*: "paid in full." When Jesus cried "It is finished," he was declaring that the debt of sin had been paid in full. The ledger was cleared. The account was settled. Nothing remained outstanding.

What was finished? Everything that needed to be done for salvation:

The work the Father had given him to do: "I glorified You on the earth, having accomplished the work which You have given Me to do."

The sacrifice for sins: "But He, having offered one sacrifice for sins for all time, sat down at the right hand of God . . . For by one offering He has perfected for all time those who are sanctified."

The redemption of sinners: "Not through the blood of goats and calves, but through His own blood, He entered the holy place once for all, having obtained eternal redemption."

The cancellation of debt: "When you were dead in your transgressions . . . He made you alive together with Him, having forgiven us all our transgressions, having canceled out the certificate of debt consisting of decrees against us, which was hostile to us; and He has taken it out of the way, having nailed it to the cross."

"Having nailed it to the cross." The record of your sins—the list of every wrong you have ever done or will ever do—was nailed to the cross with Jesus. It has been canceled, taken out of the way, paid in full. *Tetelestai.*

At the moment of Jesus's death, something remarkable happened: "The veil of the temple was torn in two from top to bottom." This veil had separated the Holy of Holies—the presence of God—from the rest of the temple. Only the high priest could enter, and only once a year. But when Jesus died, the veil was ripped apart. Access to God was opened. The barrier was removed.

> *"Therefore, brethren, since we have confidence to enter the holy place by the blood of Jesus, by a new and living way which He inaugurated for us through the veil, that is, His flesh . . . "* (Heb 10:19–20)

Through the blood of Jesus, we have "confidence to enter the holy place." The way is open. The work is done. It is finished.

THE CROSS AND YOU

The cross is not merely an event in history. It is an event with implications for you, personally, today.

> *"But God demonstrates His own love toward us, in that while we were yet sinners, Christ died for us."* (Rom 5:8)

"Christ died for us." For you. The cross is God's love demonstrated, displayed, proven beyond all doubt. You can know that God loves you because you can look at the cross and see what that love cost him.

> *"In this is love, not that we loved God, but that He loved us and sent His Son to be the propitiation for our sins."* (1 John 4:10)

"In this is love." If you want to know what love is, look at the cross. This is love defined, measured, proven. Not our love for God—that came after. But his love for us—the love that gave when we deserved nothing but judgment.

The apostle Paul made this deeply personal:

> *"I have been crucified with Christ; and it is no longer I who live, but Christ lives in me; and the life which I now live in the flesh I live by faith in the Son of God, who loved me and gave Himself up for me."* (Gal 2:20)

"Who loved *me* and gave Himself up for *me*." This is not abstract theology. This is intensely personal. The Son of God loved Paul—and gave himself for Paul. And the same is true for you. He loved you. He gave himself for you. The cross was for you.

> *"To Him who loves us and released us from our sins by His blood . . . "* (Rev 1:5)

> *"Or do you not know that your body is a temple of the Holy Spirit who is in you, whom you have from God, and that you are not your own? For you have been bought with a price: therefore glorify God in your body."* (1 Cor 6:19–20)

"You have been bought with a price." The cross is that price. You are that valuable to God. He considered you worth the death of his Son.

How should you respond to such love? The old hymn writer Isaac Watts captured it perfectly:

> *When I survey the wondrous cross*
> *On which the Prince of glory died,*
> *My richest gain I count but loss,*
> *And pour contempt on all my pride.* (Isaac Watts, 1707)

The only appropriate response to the cross is the surrender of everything. When you see what the gift cost, nothing you have seems too precious to give back.

QUESTIONS FOR REFLECTION

- Before reading this chapter, how did you think about the cross? Has your understanding deepened or changed?
- What does it mean to you that Jesus was your substitute—that he took the punishment you deserved?
- How does understanding God's wrath help you appreciate the cross? Why is it important that God is both just and loving?
- Jesus cried "*Tetelestai*"—"It is finished." What does it mean for your life that the work of salvation is complete?
- "You have been bought with a price." How should this truth affect the way you live?

A PRAYER

Lord Jesus, I stand in awe of the cross. I see what my sin cost you. I see the price you paid for my redemption. You were pierced for my transgressions. You were crushed for my iniquities. The punishment that brought me peace was upon you—and by your wounds I am healed. You who knew no sin became sin for me, so that I might become the righteousness of God. How can I ever thank you? How can I ever repay such love? I cannot—and you do not ask me to. You ask only that I receive what you have done, that I trust in the finished work of the cross, that I rest in your cry of "It is finished." I do trust you. I do rest in you. I give you everything I am, because you gave everything for me. Thank you for the cross. Thank you for your blood. Thank you for loving me when I was still your enemy. I am yours—bought with a price. Help me to live for your glory.

Amen.

PART THREE

THE RESPONSE GOD REQUIRES

". . . that whoever believes in Him . . ."

—John 3:16c

7

" . . . That Whoever Believes . . . "

What Faith Means

"Believe in the Lord Jesus, and you will be saved."

—Acts 16:31

THE HINGE OF JOHN 3:16

"For God so loved the world, that He gave His only begotten Son, that whoever believes in Him shall not perish, but have eternal life."

We have spent six chapters examining what God has done. He loved. He gave. He sent his only begotten Son to die on the cross for sinners. All of this is God's initiative, God's action, God's gift.

But now the verse turns. Now we come to the human response. Now we discover what is required of us. And the word that makes all the difference is this: *believes.*

"Whoever believes." This is the hinge of John 3:16. On one side stands everything God has done—his love, his gift, his Son, the cross. On the other side stands everything God promises—escape from perishing, eternal life. And between them stands this single word: *believes.*

Faith is the connecting link. Faith is the bridge. Faith is how the gift becomes yours.

THE UNIVERSAL INVITATION

Before we examine what it means to believe, notice the word that comes before it: *whoever.*

The Greek phrase is *pas ho pisteuōn*—"everyone who believes." This is not a restricted offer. It is thrown open as wide as humanity itself: *whoever.*[1]

This word echoes throughout Scripture:

> *"The Spirit and the bride say, 'Come.' And let the one who hears say, 'Come.' And let the one who is thirsty come; let the one who wishes take the water of life without cost."* (Rev 22:17)
>
> *"Ho! Every one who thirsts, come to the waters; and you who have no money come, buy and eat."* (Isa 55:1)
>
> *"Come to Me, all who are weary and heavy-laden, and I will give you rest."* (Matt 11:28)
>
> *"If anyone is thirsty, let him come to Me and drink."* (John 7:37)
>
> *"The one who comes to Me I will certainly not cast out."* (John 6:37)
>
> *"For 'whoever will call on the name of the Lord will be saved.'"* (Rom 10:13)

"Whoever." "Everyone." "All." "Anyone." The invitation is universal. On the day of Pentecost, Peter proclaimed: "Everyone who calls on the name of the Lord will be saved." Paul wrote: "For I am not ashamed of the gospel, for it is the power of God for salvation to *everyone* who believes."

> *"For the Scripture says, 'Whoever believes in Him will not be disappointed.' For there is no distinction between Jew*

1. The Greek phrase pas ho pisteuōn (πᾶς ὁ πιστεύων) literally means "all the believing one" or "everyone who believes."

> *and Greek; for the same Lord is Lord of all, abounding in riches for all who call on Him."* (Rom 10:11–13)

"No distinction." This means the invitation includes *you*. Whatever you have done, wherever you have been—you are included in "whoever." The door is open. The question is simply whether you will believe.

THE MEANING OF "BELIEVES"

The Greek word translated "believes" is *pisteuō* (πιστεύω). It is one of the most important words in the New Testament, appearing nearly 250 times. John's Gospel alone uses it 98 times.

Pisteuō encompasses several dimensions. It can mean to believe that something is true (intellectual assent). It can mean to trust someone (personal reliance). And in John's Gospel, it often carries the sense of commitment—to believe *into* someone, not merely to believe *about* them.

WHAT FAITH IS NOT

Faith Is Not Mere Intellectual Assent

It is possible to believe certain facts about Jesus without truly believing *in* Jesus. The demons believe that God exists—they even shudder—but they are not saved.

> *"Now when He was in Jerusalem at the Passover, during the feast, many believed in His name, observing His signs which He was doing. But Jesus, on His part, was not entrusting Himself to them, for He knew all men."* (John 2:23–24)

Many "believed"—but Jesus did not entrust himself to them. Their faith was superficial, based on signs rather than genuine commitment.

> *"Not everyone who says to Me, 'Lord, Lord,' will enter the kingdom of heaven, but he who does the will of My Father who is in heaven. Many will say to Me on that day, 'Lord,*

> *Lord, did we not prophesy in Your name?' And then I will declare to them, 'I never knew you.'"* (Matt 7:21–23)

In John 8, people who "believed" Jesus later heard him say: "You are of your father the devil." John explained: "They went out from us, but they were not really of us."

True faith persists. True faith continues. True faith is more than momentary mental assent.

Faith Is Not a Feeling

Faith is not an emotion. It is not a warm feeling in your heart or a mystical experience. Many people wait to "feel" saved. But this puts the cart before the horse.

Faith is directed toward God and his promises, not toward our feelings. The question is not "Do I feel forgiven?" but "Has God promised to forgive those who believe?"

> *"And without faith it is impossible to please Him, for he who comes to God must believe that He is and that He is a rewarder of those who seek Him."* (Heb 11:6)

True faith often exists alongside doubt. The father of the demon-possessed boy cried: "I do believe; help my unbelief." Peter stepped out in faith, then began to sink. The disciples asked, "Increase our faith!"

Faith Is Not a Good Work

Some people think of faith as a work—something we do to earn God's favor. But faith is the opposite of works. Faith is the empty hand that receives what God freely gives.

> *"For by grace you have been saved through faith; and that not of yourselves, it is the gift of God; not as a result of works, so that no one may boast."* (Eph 2:8–9)

> *"Because by the works of the Law no flesh will be justified in His sight."* (Rom 3:20)

> *"For we maintain that a man is justified by faith apart from works of the Law."* (Rom 3:28)
>
> *"He saved us, not on the basis of deeds which we have done in righteousness, but according to His mercy."* (Titus 3:5)
>
> *"Now to the one who works, his wage is not credited as a favor, but as what is due. But to the one who does not work, but believes in Him who justifies the ungodly, his faith is credited as righteousness."* (Rom 4:4–5)

"To the one who *does not work*, but *believes*." Faith and works are contrasted, not combined. Faith is the channel through which grace flows—not a contribution we make.

WHAT FAITH IS

The word *pisteuō* carries three dimensions: knowledge, assent, and trust.

Faith Involves Knowledge

Saving faith is not blind. It is based on knowledge—on facts about who Jesus is and what he has done. You cannot believe in Jesus if you know nothing about him.

Faith Involves Assent

Faith involves agreement—believing that certain things are true. "Yes, Jesus is who he claimed to be. Yes, he died for my sins. Yes, salvation is found in him alone."

> *"Now faith is the assurance of things hoped for, the conviction of things not seen."* (Heb 11:1)

Faith Involves Trust

Saving faith goes beyond knowledge and assent to *trust*—personal reliance on Christ for salvation. This is the heart of biblical faith.

You can believe that a chair will hold your weight (knowledge and assent) without actually sitting in it (trust). Saving faith is actually sitting down, actually committing yourself to Christ.

> *"But as many as received Him, to them He gave the right to become children of God, even to those who believe in His name."* (John 1:12)

Notice the parallel: "received Him" and "believe in His name" are used synonymously. To believe is to receive.

FAITH IN ACTION

What does faith look like in practice? Jesus described it in various ways:

> *"Truly, truly, I say to you, he who hears My word, and believes Him who sent Me, has eternal life."* (John 5:24)

Faith is *hearing* Christ's word and *believing* the Father.

> *"I am the bread of life; he who comes to Me will not hunger, and he who believes in Me will never thirst."* (John 6:35)

Faith is *coming* to Jesus.

> *"I am the door; if anyone enters through Me, he will be saved."* (John 10:9)

Faith is *entering* through Jesus.

> *"Believe in the Lord Jesus, and you will be saved."* (Acts 16:31)
>
> *"If you confess with your mouth Jesus as Lord, and believe in your heart that God raised Him from the dead, you will be saved."* (Rom 10:9)

BIBLICAL EXAMPLES OF FAITH

Abraham is the preeminent example. "By faith Abraham, when he was called, obeyed by going out to a place which he was to receive for an inheritance; and he went out, not knowing where he was going."

What did God count as righteousness? Not Abraham's works, but his faith: "Abraham believed God, and it was credited to him as righteousness."

> *"In hope against hope he believed . . . being fully assured that what God had promised, He was able also to perform."* (Rom 4:18, 21)

The royal official in John 4: Jesus said, "Go; your son lives." And "The man believed the word that Jesus spoke to him and started off."

The centurion amazed Jesus: "Just say the word, and my servant will be healed." Jesus responded: "I have not found such great faith with anyone in Israel."

Thomas moved from doubt to faith: "My Lord and my God!" Jesus replied: "Blessed are they who did not see, and yet believed."

FAITH ALONE

The Reformers summarized biblical teaching with *sola fide*—"by faith alone." This means faith is the *sole instrument* by which we receive salvation.

> *"But now apart from the Law the righteousness of God has been manifested . . . even the righteousness of God through faith in Jesus Christ for all those who believe."* (Rom 3:21–22)
>
> *"Therefore, having been justified by faith, we have peace with God through our Lord Jesus Christ."* (Rom 5:1)
>
> *"Now that no one is justified by the Law before God is evident; for, 'The righteous man shall live by faith.'"* (Gal 3:11)

"The righteous shall live by faith." This Old Testament quotation appears four times in the New Testament. It is the heartbeat of the gospel.

> *"More than that, I count all things to be loss in view of the surpassing value of knowing Christ Jesus my Lord . . . not having a righteousness of my own derived from the Law, but that which is through faith in Christ."* (Phil 3:8–9)

FAITH AND WORKS: GETTING THE RELATIONSHIP RIGHT

But what about James? Does he not say that faith without works is dead?

James and Paul are not contradicting each other. Paul asks: "How is a person justified before God?" Answer: by faith alone. James asks: "How do we know if faith is genuine?" Answer: genuine faith produces works.

Faith is the root; works are the fruit. You are not saved *by* the fruit, but you are saved *for* the fruit.

> *"For we are His workmanship, created in Christ Jesus for good works, which God prepared beforehand so that we would walk in them."* (Eph 2:10)
>
> *"For in Christ Jesus neither circumcision nor uncircumcision means anything, but faith working through love."* (Gal 5:6)
>
> *"What shall we say then? Are we to continue in sin so that grace may increase? May it never be!"* (Rom 6:1–2)

True faith produces transformation. Saving faith bears fruit—not perfect fruit, but real evidence that new life has begun.

THE URGENCY OF FAITH

John 3:16 does not present faith as optional. It is the sole condition for receiving eternal life.

> *"He who believes in the Son has eternal life; but he who does not obey the Son will not see life, but the wrath of God abides on him."* (John 3:36)
>
> *"Therefore I said to you that you will die in your sins; for unless you believe that I am He, you will die in your sins."* (John 8:24)
>
> *"And without faith it is impossible to please Him."* (Heb 11:6)

"Impossible to please Him." Without faith, you cannot please God. Faith is not one option among many. Jesus began his ministry: "Repent and believe in the gospel."

Will you believe?

QUESTIONS FOR REFLECTION

- Before reading this chapter, how would you have defined "faith"? Has your understanding changed?
- What is the difference between believing facts about Jesus and trusting in Jesus?
- Why is it important to understand that faith is not a work?
- The word "whoever" means the invitation is open to you. What is preventing you from trusting Christ completely?
- If genuine faith produces good works, what evidence of faith do you see in your life?

A PRAYER

Lord Jesus, I confess that I have often misunderstood what it means to believe. I have treated faith as mere mental agreement, as an emotional experience, or as something I must achieve. But I see now that faith is simpler—and deeper—than I realized. It is trusting you. It is receiving what you offer. I do not come with impressive works or religious credentials. I come empty-handed. And you have said that whoever comes to you, you will not cast out. So I come. I believe—help my unbelief. I trust you as my Savior. I receive you as my Lord. Not on my feelings, not on my efforts, but on you. Thank you that 'whoever believes' includes me.

Amen.

8

" . . . In Him . . . "
The Object of Faith

"Lord, to whom shall we go? You have words of eternal life."

—John 6:68

THE IMPORTANCE OF "IN HIM"

"Whoever believes in Him." We have explored what it means to believe. But believe in whom? This is the crucial question. Faith is only as good as its object.[1]

The Greek phrase is *eis auton*—literally, "into him." This is not faith in general. It is not faith in faith. It is not faith in religion, in good intentions, in sincerity, or in ourselves. It is faith *in Him*—in Jesus Christ, the Son of God.

A person can have great faith in the wrong object and be lost. Another can have weak, trembling faith in the right object and be saved. What makes faith saving is not the strength of the faith but the worth of the One in whom faith is placed.

1. The Greek verb pisteuō (πιστεύω) appears 98 times in John's Gospel—more than in Matthew, Mark, and Luke combined.

Consider this illustration: A man walks confidently onto thin ice, certain it will hold him. His faith is strong, but his object is weak—and he falls through. Another man trembles as he steps onto thick ice, barely daring to trust it. His faith is weak, but his object is strong—and he crosses safely. The first man's confidence could not save him. The second man's doubt could not sink him. Everything depended on the object of their trust.

So it is with saving faith. You can sincerely believe in something false and be lost forever. Or you can come to Christ with faltering, uncertain faith—and be saved eternally. The question is not "How strong is your faith?" but "In whom do you believe?"

NOT FAITH IN FAITH

Our culture celebrates faith as a virtue in itself. "Just believe," people say. "Have faith." "Believe in yourself." But faith without a worthy object is worthless—or worse, dangerous.

Jesus never said, "Just believe." He said, "Believe in God, believe also in *Me*." The apostles never said, "Have faith." They said, "Believe in the *Lord Jesus*, and you will be saved."

Paul asked the pointed question: "How then will they call on Him in whom they have not believed? And how will they believe in Him *of whom they have not heard*?" Faith requires content. It requires knowledge of the One in whom we believe. It must have an object—and that object must be Christ.

The writer of Hebrews calls us to fix our eyes "on Jesus, the author and perfecter of faith." Jesus is not merely the model of faith; he is the object of faith, the origin of faith, and the goal of faith. Everything centers on him.

When many disciples were turning away from Jesus, he asked the Twelve: "You do not want to go away also, do you?" Peter answered for them all: "Lord, to whom shall we go? *You have words of eternal life*. We have believed and have come to know that You are the Holy One of God." Peter understood: there is no alternative. It is Christ or nothing.

LOOK AND LIVE

The Old Testament provides a powerful picture of what it means to believe "in Him." God told Israel through Isaiah:

> *"Turn to Me and be saved, all the ends of the earth; for I am God, and there is no other."* (Isa 45:22)

"Turn to *Me*." Salvation is found by looking to God, by turning to him, by trusting in him alone. But how would God accomplish this salvation? Through his Son.

In the wilderness, when poisonous serpents bit the Israelites and many were dying, God commanded Moses: "Make a fiery serpent, and set it on a standard; and it shall come about, that everyone who is bitten, when he looks at it, he will live."

The remedy was simple: look and live. Not work and live. Not earn and live. Not understand and live. Simply look at what God had provided—and live.

Jesus himself applied this very story to his own saving work:

> *"As Moses lifted up the serpent in the wilderness, even so must the Son of Man be lifted up; so that whoever believes will in Him have eternal life."* (John 3:14–15)

Jesus is the One lifted up. Jesus is the remedy for the serpent's bite of sin. Whoever looks to him in faith—whoever believes in him—will have eternal life. The object of faith is everything.

WHO IS THIS "HIM"?

If the object of faith is everything, then we must know clearly *who* this "him" is. John's Gospel has already told us. The Son in whom we must believe is:

The Eternal Word

> *"In the beginning was the Word, and the Word was with God, and the Word was God."* (John 1:1)

Before anything was created, he already existed. He was with God and he was God. This is not a created being, not an angel, not a mere man. This is God himself—the eternal Son, the second Person of the Trinity.

The Incarnate One

> *"And the Word became flesh, and dwelt among us, and we saw His glory, glory as of the only begotten from the Father, full of grace and truth."* (John 1:14)

The eternal Word took on human flesh. He "dwelt among us"—literally, "tabernacled" among us, as God's presence once dwelt in the tabernacle. He is the true meeting place between God and humanity. "No one has ever seen God; the only begotten God who is in the bosom of the Father, He has explained Him."

The Humble Servant

> *"Who, although He existed in the form of God, did not regard equality with God a thing to be grasped, but emptied Himself, taking the form of a bond-servant, and being made in the likeness of men. Being found in appearance as a man, He humbled Himself by becoming obedient to the point of death, even death on a cross."* (Phil 2:6–8)

He who was equal with God became a servant. He who was rich became poor. He who was exalted humbled himself to the lowest point imaginable—death on a cross.

The Creator and Sustainer

> *"He is the image of the invisible God, the firstborn of all creation. For by Him all things were created, both in the heavens and on earth, visible and invisible, whether thrones or dominions or rulers or authorities—all things have been*

> *created through Him and for Him. He is before all things, and in Him all things hold together."* (Col 1:15–17)

This is no ordinary man. This is the Creator of the universe, the One who holds all things together by the word of his power. He is the One who upholds all things, "the radiance of God's glory and the exact representation of His nature."

The Great I AM

Jesus claimed the divine name for himself. When challenged about his identity, he declared: "Truly, truly, I say to you, before Abraham was born, *I am*." He said, "I and the Father are one." When Thomas saw the risen Christ, he fell down and worshiped: "My Lord and my God!"

This is the "Him" of John 3:16. This is the object of saving faith. Not a mere teacher. Not a moral example. Not a religious figure among many. God himself, come in the flesh to save sinners.

THE NAMES THAT REVEAL HIM

The names given to Jesus in Scripture reveal who he is and why he alone is worthy of our faith.

Jesus—The Savior

The angel announced to Joseph: "She will bear a Son; and you shall call His name Jesus, for He will save His people from their sins." The name "Jesus" means "Yahweh saves" or "Yahweh is salvation." His very name declares his mission: to save.

> *"For today in the city of David there has been born for you a Savior, who is Christ the Lord."* (Luke 2:11)

The apostles proclaimed him as "Prince and Savior, to grant repentance to Israel, and forgiveness of sins." Paul called him "our great God and Savior, Christ Jesus."

The Samaritans who believed in Jesus declared: "This One is indeed the Savior of the world." John confirmed: "We have seen and testify that the Father has sent the Son to be the Savior of the world."

> *"And there is salvation in no one else; for there is no other name under heaven that has been given among men by which we must be saved."* (Acts 4:12)

"No other name." Not Buddha. Not Muhammad. Not any religious leader or system. Only Jesus. Only this name. Why? Because only this Savior actually saves. Others point the way; he *is* the way. Others teach truth; he *is* the truth. Others speak of life; he *is* the life.

Christ—The Anointed One

"Christ" is not Jesus's last name. It is a title—the Greek translation of the Hebrew "Messiah," meaning "Anointed One." In the Old Testament, prophets, priests, and kings were anointed with oil as a sign of God's calling and empowerment. Jesus is all three: the Prophet who speaks God's word, the Priest who offers himself as sacrifice, and the King who rules forever.

Isaiah prophesied of him: "The Spirit of the Lord GOD is upon me, because the LORD has anointed me to bring good news to the afflicted."

Peter confessed: "You are the Christ, the Son of the living God." Martha declared: "Yes, Lord; I have believed that You are the Christ, the Son of God, even He who comes into the world."

John stated the purpose of his entire Gospel: "These have been written so that you may believe that Jesus is the Christ, the Son of God; and that believing you may have life in His name."

Son of God—The Divine King

"Son of God" was a messianic title rooted in God's promise to David. God promised that David's descendant would reign forever, and God declared of him: "I will be a father to him, and he will be a son to Me." Psalm 2 proclaimed: "You are My Son, today I have begotten You."

But for Jesus, "Son of God" meant more than messianic kingship. It meant unique relationship with the Father, sharing his divine nature. The Father's voice from heaven declared: "This is My beloved Son, in whom I am well-pleased." The writer of Hebrews applied Psalm 2 to Jesus: "For to which of the angels did He ever say, 'You are My Son, today I have begotten You'?"

The Jews understood exactly what Jesus meant when he called God his Father. "For this reason therefore the Jews were seeking all the more to kill Him, because He not only was breaking the Sabbath, but also was calling God His own Father, *making Himself equal with God.*"

Jesus declared himself the eternal Son of God, equal with the Father. Paul wrote: "He was declared the Son of God with power by the resurrection from the dead."

Lord—The Sovereign Master

> *"For this reason also, God highly exalted Him, and bestowed on Him the name which is above every name, so that at the name of Jesus every knee will bow, of those who are in heaven and on earth and under the earth, and that every tongue will confess that Jesus Christ is Lord, to the glory of God the Father."* (Phil 2:9–11)

"Lord" (*kurios*) is the title used in the Greek Old Testament to translate the divine name YHWH. When the early Christians called Jesus "Lord," they were affirming his deity. He is not merely a teacher or master in the human sense; he is the Lord God.

The essential Christian confession is: "Jesus is Lord." Paul wrote: "No one can say, 'Jesus is Lord,' except by the Holy Spirit." Peter preached on Pentecost: "Let all the house of Israel know for certain that God has made Him both Lord and Christ—this Jesus whom you crucified."

He is the King of kings and Lord of lords. To believe "in Him" is to believe in One who has absolute authority, One who deserves total allegiance, One who will one day judge the living and the dead.

WHAT JESUS HAS DONE

To believe "in Him" means not only knowing who Jesus is but also trusting in what he has done. Faith rests on the finished work of Christ.

He Died for Our Sins

> *"Being justified as a gift by His grace through the redemption which is in Christ Jesus; whom God displayed publicly as a propitiation in His blood through faith."* (Rom 3:24–25)

This is the heart of the gospel: "Christ died for our sins according to the Scriptures." His death was not a tragedy but a triumph. It was not a defeat but a victory. On the cross, he accomplished our redemption.

"He made Him who knew no sin to be sin on our behalf, so that we might become the righteousness of God in Him." "Christ redeemed us from the curse of the Law, having become a curse for us." "He Himself bore our sins in His body on the cross, so that we might die to sin and live to righteousness."

"Christ also, having been offered once to bear the sins of many, will appear a second time for salvation without reference to sin." His sacrifice was once for all. It never needs to be repeated. It is completely sufficient.

He Rose from the Dead

Faith rests not only on Christ's death but on his resurrection. He "was delivered over because of our transgressions, and was raised because of our justification."

> *"And if Christ has not been raised, your faith is worthless; you are still in your sins."* (1 Cor 15:17)

But Christ *has* been raised! He "was declared the Son of God with power by the resurrection from the dead." God "has furnished proof to all men by raising Him from the dead." "Christ, having been raised from the dead, is never to die again; death no longer is master over Him."

The resurrection proves that the Father accepted the Son's sacrifice. It demonstrates that Jesus is who he claimed to be. It guarantees that those who trust in him will also be raised.

He Lives to Intercede

> *"Therefore He is able also to save forever those who draw near to God through Him, since He always lives to make intercession for them."* (Heb 7:25)

Jesus did not simply die and rise again. He ascended to the Father's right hand, where he now lives to intercede for his people. "Christ Jesus is He who died, yes, rather who was raised, who is at the right hand of God, who also intercedes for us."

"If anyone sins, we have an Advocate with the Father, Jesus Christ the righteous." When we fall, when we fail, when we sin, we have One who speaks in our defense. Our salvation does not depend on our ability to keep ourselves saved. It depends on Christ's ability to keep us.

> *"Therefore, since we have a great high priest who has passed through the heavens, Jesus the Son of God, let us hold fast our confession. For we do not have a high priest who cannot sympathize with our weaknesses, but One who has been tempted in all things as we are, yet without sin. Therefore let us draw near with confidence to the throne of grace, so that we may receive mercy and find grace to help in time of need."* (Heb 4:14–16)

He Will Return in Glory

Jesus promised to return. The angels announced at his ascension: "This Jesus, who has been taken up from you into heaven, will come in just the same way as you have watched Him go into heaven."

> *"For the Lord Himself will descend from heaven with a shout, with the voice of the archangel and with the trumpet of God, and the dead in Christ will rise first. Then we who are alive and remain will be caught up together with them in the clouds to meet the Lord in the air, and so we shall always be with the Lord."* (1 Thess 4:16–17)

The last prayer in the Bible is: "Come, Lord Jesus." Those who believe in him look forward to his return, when faith will become sight and hope will become reality.

WHY ONLY JESUS?

If the object of faith is so important, we must ask: Why Jesus and no other? Why must we believe "in Him" specifically?

> *"Jesus said to him, 'I am the way, and the truth, and the life; no one comes to the Father but through Me.'"* (John 14:6)
>
> *"I am the door; if anyone enters through Me, he will be saved."* (John 10:9)
>
> *"For there is one God, and one mediator also between God and men, the man Christ Jesus."* (1 Tim 2:5)

Jesus alone is qualified to save because:

He alone is sinless. "A high priest . . . holy, innocent, undefiled, separated from sinners." Only a sinless substitute could die for sinners.

He alone paid the price. "You were not redeemed with perishable things like silver or gold . . . but with precious blood, as of a lamb unblemished and spotless, the blood of Christ." No one else has made atonement for sin.

He alone conquered death. “If Christ has not been raised, your faith is worthless . . . But now Christ has been raised from the dead.” No other religious founder has risen from the dead. Only Jesus has the power to give eternal life because only Jesus has defeated death.

THE TRUSTWORTHINESS OF JESUS

Can Jesus be trusted? Can you stake your eternal destiny on him? Consider his trustworthiness:

He who gave his Son will not fail you. “He who did not spare His own Son, but delivered Him over for us all, how will He not also with Him freely give us all things?” If God gave his most precious gift, will he withhold anything we need?

He who holds you will not let you go. Jesus promised: “I give eternal life to them, and they will never perish; and no one will snatch them out of My hand. My Father, who has given them to Me, is greater than all; and no one is able to snatch them out of the Father’s hand.”

He who began will complete the work. Paul expressed this confidence: “I know whom I have believed and I am convinced that He is able to guard what I have entrusted to Him until that day.”

The question is not whether Jesus is trustworthy. He has proven himself trustworthy beyond all doubt. The question is whether you will trust him.

KNOWING HIM

Saving faith is ultimately personal. It is not merely believing facts about Christ but knowing Christ himself.

> *“This is eternal life, that they may know You, the only true God, and Jesus Christ whom You have sent.”* (John 17:3)

Notice: eternal life is defined as *knowing* God and knowing Jesus Christ. Not just knowing about them. *Knowing them*—personally, intimately, relationally.

Paul expressed his deepest desire: "That I may know Him and the power of His resurrection and the fellowship of His sufferings." He counted everything as loss "in view of the surpassing value of *knowing Christ Jesus my Lord*."

Jesus spoke of this intimate relationship: "I am the good shepherd, and I know My own and My own know Me." The shepherd knows each sheep by name. The sheep know the shepherd's voice and follow him.

Paul described the Christian life as Christ living in the believer: "I have been crucified with Christ; and it is no longer I who live, but Christ lives in me; and the life which I now live in the flesh I live by faith in the Son of God, who loved me and gave Himself up for me."

This is "Christ in you, the hope of glory." This is the vine and the branches: "I am the vine, you are the branches; he who abides in Me and I in him, he bears much fruit."

Faith is not merely intellectual agreement about Jesus. It is personal trust in Jesus. It is receiving him, coming to him, resting in him, abiding in him. It is a living relationship with the living Lord.

WILL YOU COME TO HIM?

"Whoever believes in Him." The "Him" has now been clearly identified. He is God the Son, eternal and almighty. He is Jesus the Savior, who died and rose again. He is Christ the King, anointed to rule forever. He is the Lord of all, to whom every knee will bow.

And this almighty Lord issues a tender invitation:

> *"Come to Me, all who are weary and heavy-laden, and I will give you rest."* (Matt 11:28)

He does not say, "Come to a religion." He says, "Come to Me." He does not say, "Follow a system." He says, "Follow Me." He does not say, "Believe a creed." He says, "Believe in Me."

This is profoundly personal. Jesus invites you to himself. He offers himself as your Savior, your Lord, your Life. He asks you to trust not in something but in Someone—in him.

Do you know this Jesus? Not just know about him—do you know him? Have you come to him? Have you put your faith in him—not in your own goodness, not in religious rituals, not in vague spirituality, but in the living Christ?

He is worthy of your trust. He will not disappoint you. Come to him today.

QUESTIONS FOR REFLECTION

- Why is the object of faith more important than the strength of faith? What does this mean for those who feel their faith is weak?
- How would you explain to someone who Jesus is, using his names and titles?
- Why can no other religious figure save us? What makes Jesus uniquely qualified?
- What is the difference between believing facts about Jesus and knowing Jesus personally?
- Jesus invites you to come to him personally. How will you respond to his invitation?

A PRAYER

Lord Jesus Christ, Son of God, Savior of the world—I come to you. Not to a religion, not to a system, not to a set of rules—but to you, the living Lord. I believe that you are who you claimed to be: the eternal Son of God who became man for my salvation. I believe what you have done: you died for my sins, you rose from the dead, you live to intercede for me. I trust you as my Savior. I receive you as my Lord. I rest my entire hope on you and you alone. You are worthy of all my trust. You have proven yourself faithful. Into your hands I commit my life, my soul, my eternal destiny. Hold me fast. Guard what I have entrusted to you. Never let me go. And bring me safely to your Father's house, where I will see you face to face and know you fully, even as I am fully known.

Amen.

9

Repentance
The Other Side of Faith

"Repent and believe in the gospel."

—Mark 1:15

THE MISSING WORD

We have spent two chapters exploring what it means to believe. But there is another word that belongs alongside faith—a word that is often neglected or misunderstood in our time. That word is *repentance.*

John 3:16 speaks of believing. But the verse immediately before it speaks of being "born again," and the verses that follow speak of coming to the light so that one's deeds may be exposed. The call to believe does not exist in isolation. It is part of a larger call to turn from darkness to light, from sin to the Savior.

Jesus began his public ministry with these words:

> *"The time is fulfilled, and the kingdom of God is at hand; repent and believe in the gospel."* (Mark 1:15)

"Repent *and* believe." Not repent *or* believe. Not believe without repenting. The two go together. They are two sides of the same coin, two aspects of the same response to God.

You cannot truly believe in Christ while clinging to your sin. And you cannot truly repent of sin without turning to Christ in faith. Faith and repentance are inseparable. As the Puritan Thomas Watson wrote, "Repentance and faith are two wings by which we fly to heaven."

WHAT REPENTANCE MEANS

The Greek word for repentance is *metanoia* (μετάνοια). It is formed from *meta* (μετά, "after" or "change") and *nous* (νοῦς, "mind"). Literally, it means a "change of mind" or "afterthought." But in biblical usage, it means far more than merely changing your opinion. It means a fundamental transformation of your thinking that results in a complete change of direction.[1]

In the Old Testament, the Hebrew word most often translated "repent" is *shuv* (שׁוּב), which means "to turn" or "to return." The prophets repeatedly called Israel to turn back to God:

> *"Return to Me," declares the LORD of hosts, "and I will return to you."* (Zech 1:3)
>
> *"Return, O Israel, to the LORD your God, for you have stumbled because of your iniquity."* (Hos 14:1)
>
> *"Return to Me, and I will return to you," says the LORD of hosts.* (Mal 3:7)
>
> *"Repent and turn away from all your transgressions, so that iniquity may not become a stumbling block to you."* (Ezek 18:30)

Repentance, then, involves a turning—a complete about-face. It means turning *from* sin and turning *to* God. It is not merely feeling bad about your sin; it is abandoning your sin and embracing God.

1. The Greek noun metanoia (μετάνοια) and verb metanoeō (μετανοέω) derive from meta ("after, change") and nous ("mind").

THE ELEMENTS OF TRUE REPENTANCE

True repentance involves the whole person—mind, emotions, and will.

A Change of Mind

First, there must be a change in how you *think*. You come to see sin as God sees it—not as a minor failing, not as an acceptable weakness, but as rebellion against the holy God. You recognize that your way has been wrong and God's way is right.

The prodigal son illustrates this. Scripture says he "came to his senses" and said:

> *"I will get up and go to my father, and will say to him, 'Father, I have sinned against heaven, and in your sight; I am no longer worthy to be called your son.'"* (Luke 15:17–19)

He stopped making excuses. He stopped justifying his choices. He acknowledged the truth about himself and about his father.

A Change of Heart

Second, there must be a change in how you *feel*. True repentance involves genuine sorrow for sin—not merely sorrow for being caught, not merely regret for consequences, but grief over having offended God.

Paul distinguished between two kinds of sorrow:

> *"For the sorrow that is according to the will of God produces a repentance without regret, leading to salvation, but the sorrow of the world produces death."* (2 Cor 7:10)

"Worldly sorrow" is merely feeling bad about consequences. "Godly sorrow" is grieving because you have sinned against a holy and loving God. One leads to death; the other leads to life.

David expressed this godly sorrow in his great psalm of repentance:

> *"Against You, You only, I have sinned and done what is evil in Your sight, so that You are justified when You speak and blameless when You judge."* (Ps 51:4)

David had sinned against Bathsheba, against Uriah, against his family, against his nation. Yet he recognized that ultimately all sin is against God. This recognition breaks the heart.

A Change of Will

Third, there must be a change in what you *choose*. True repentance involves the will—a deliberate decision to turn from sin and turn to God. It is not enough to think differently or feel differently; you must *act* differently.

The prodigal son did not merely come to his senses; Scripture says, "He got up and came to his father." His change of mind led to a change of direction. He left the far country and went home.

John the Baptist demanded evidence of genuine repentance:

> *"Therefore bear fruit in keeping with repentance."* (Matt 3:8)

True repentance produces fruit. It shows itself in changed behavior. A tree is known by its fruit, and repentance is known by its results.

WHAT REPENTANCE IS NOT

To understand what repentance is, we must also understand what it is not.

Repentance Is Not Mere Regret

Many people feel sorry for their sins without ever truly repenting. Judas "felt remorse" after betraying Jesus:

> *"Then when Judas, who had betrayed Him, saw that He had been condemned, he felt remorse and returned the thirty pieces of silver to the chief priests and elders."* (Matt 27:3)

But his remorse led only to despair and suicide, not to salvation. He regretted what he had done, but he did not turn to God for forgiveness.

Regret says, "I wish I hadn't done that." Repentance says, "I was wrong, God is right, and I am turning to Him."

Repentance Is Not Penance

Repentance is not something you do to pay for your sins or earn God's favor. You cannot balance the scales by punishing yourself, performing religious duties, or making up for past wrongs. The whole point of the gospel is that Jesus paid for your sins because you could not.

> *"He saved us, not on the basis of deeds which we have done in righteousness, but according to His mercy, by the washing of regeneration and renewing by the Holy Spirit."* (Titus 3:5–6)

Penance says, "I must do something to make things right." Repentance says, "I cannot make things right—only Christ can—and I am trusting in Him."

Repentance Is Not Self-Improvement

Repentance is not a self-help program. It is not resolving to do better, turning over a new leaf, or making New Year's resolutions. These efforts rely on human willpower and inevitably fail.

Self-improvement says, "I will try harder." Repentance says, "I cannot save myself—I need a Savior."

True repentance recognizes that the problem is not merely bad habits that need correction but a sinful heart that needs transformation. And that transformation can only come from God:

> *"Create in me a clean heart, O God, and renew a steadfast spirit within me."* (Ps 51:10)

Repentance Is Not Perfect Performance

Some people believe they cannot repent until they can guarantee they will never sin again. But this misunderstands repentance. Repentance is a change of direction, not a claim to perfection.

When you board a plane from New York to Los Angeles, you commit to traveling west. The plane may encounter turbulence; it may need to adjust course; it may even circle back briefly. But the fundamental direction remains westward. So it is with repentance. You turn from sin and toward God. You will stumble; you will need to repent again. But the direction of your life has changed.

BIBLICAL EXAMPLES OF REPENTANCE

Scripture gives us powerful portraits of what true repentance looks like.

The Prodigal Son

Jesus's parable of the prodigal son is the greatest picture of repentance in Scripture. The younger son demanded his inheritance, left home, and squandered everything in reckless living. When he found himself starving among pigs, "he came to his senses."

Notice the elements of his repentance: He recognized his sin ("I have sinned against heaven and in your sight"). He acknowledged his unworthiness ("I am no longer worthy to be called your son"). And he acted—"he got up and came to his father."

Notice too the father's response:

> *"But while he was still a long way off, his father saw him and felt compassion for him, and ran and embraced him and kissed him."* (Luke 15:20)

The father did not wait for a perfect apology or demand that the son prove himself. He welcomed him home with joy. This is how God receives repentant sinners.

King David

David committed adultery with Bathsheba and arranged the murder of her husband Uriah. For nearly a year, he hid his sin. Then the prophet Nathan confronted him, and David confessed:

> *"I have sinned against the LORD."* (2 Sam 12:13)

Psalm 51 records David's prayer of repentance. It reveals the depth of genuine repentance:

> *"Be gracious to me, O God, according to Your lovingkindness; according to the greatness of Your compassion blot out my transgressions. Wash me thoroughly from my iniquity and cleanse me from my sin. For I know my transgressions, and my sin is ever before me."* (Ps 51:1–2)

David did not minimize his sin or make excuses. He acknowledged that he deserved judgment. And he cast himself entirely on God's mercy.

The Tax Collector

In Jesus's parable of the Pharisee and the tax collector, we see two men praying in the temple. The Pharisee listed his religious accomplishments:

> *"God, I thank You that I am not like other people: swindlers, unjust, adulterers, or even like this tax collector. I fast twice a week; I pay tithes of all that I get."* (Luke 18:11–12)

But the tax collector:

> *"Was even unwilling to lift up his eyes to heaven, but was beating his breast, saying, 'God, be merciful to me, the sinner!'"* (Luke 18:13)

Jesus said the tax collector "went to his house justified." Why? Because he came to God with nothing to offer except his need. He did not compare himself to others. He did not point to his achievements. He simply acknowledged his sin and pleaded for mercy.

This is the posture of true repentance.

Zacchaeus

Zacchaeus was a chief tax collector—wealthy, corrupt, and despised. When Jesus called him down from the sycamore tree and went to his house, Zacchaeus's life was transformed:

> *"Zacchaeus stopped and said to the Lord, 'Behold, Lord, half of my possessions I will give to the poor, and if I have defrauded anyone of anything, I will give back four times as much.'"* (Luke 19:8)

Jesus responded:

> *"Today salvation has come to this house."* (Luke 19:9)

Zacchaeus's repentance was demonstrated by radical action. The man who had lived for money now gave it away. His changed behavior proved his changed heart.

The Ninevites

When Jonah finally preached to Nineveh, the entire city repented—from the king to the commoner. The king issued a decree:

> *"Let men call on God earnestly that each may turn from his wicked way and from the violence which is in his hands. Who knows, God may turn and relent and withdraw His burning anger so that we will not perish."* (Jonah 3:8–9)

And God did relent. Jesus later said that the Ninevites "repented at the preaching of Jonah" and would rise up in judgment against the unrepentant generation of his day. Even the most wicked city can be transformed by genuine repentance.

THE FRUIT OF REPENTANCE

How do you know if repentance is genuine? By its fruit. John the Baptist warned the religious leaders:

> *"You brood of vipers, who warned you to flee from the wrath to come? Therefore bear fruit in keeping with repentance."* (Matt 3:7–8)

When the crowds asked what this fruit looked like, John gave practical examples:

> *"The man who has two tunics is to share with him who has none; and he who has food is to do likewise."* (Luke 3:11)

To tax collectors: "Collect no more than what you have been ordered to." To soldiers: "Do not take money from anyone by force, or accuse anyone falsely, and be content with your wages."

Paul described the same reality to King Agrippa:

> *"I kept declaring both to those of Damascus first, and also at Jerusalem and then throughout all the region of Judea, and even to the Gentiles, that they should repent and turn to God, performing deeds appropriate to repentance."* (Acts 26:20)

"Deeds appropriate to repentance." True repentance is visible. It produces change. Not perfect change—but real change. Not overnight transformation—but a new direction that persists and grows.

The fruit of repentance includes:

Confession of sin—acknowledging specific sins to God and, where appropriate, to others.

Forsaking sin—making deliberate choices to avoid temptation and walk in obedience.

Restitution where possible—seeking to repair damage caused by sin, as Zacchaeus did.

A changed life pattern—new habits, new priorities, new relationships that reflect the reality of new life in Christ.

REPENTANCE AND FAITH TOGETHER

Throughout the New Testament, repentance and faith are presented together as the proper response to the gospel.

Jesus proclaimed:

> *"Repent and believe in the gospel."* (Mark 1:15)

Peter preached on Pentecost:

> *"Repent, and each of you be baptized in the name of Jesus Christ for the forgiveness of your sins; and you will receive the gift of the Holy Spirit."* (Acts 2:38)

Paul summarized his ministry:

> *"Solemnly testifying to both Jews and Greeks of repentance toward God and faith in our Lord Jesus Christ."* (Acts 20:21)

"Repentance toward God and faith in our Lord Jesus Christ." These are not two separate steps but two aspects of one turning. You cannot truly turn to Christ (faith) without turning from sin (repentance). And you cannot truly turn from sin (repentance) without turning to Christ (faith).

Think of it this way: If you are walking north and need to go south, you must do two things simultaneously. You must turn *away from* the north, and you must turn *toward* the south. You cannot do one without the other. It is one turn with two aspects.

So it is with coming to Christ. Repentance is turning from sin; faith is turning to the Savior. Together they constitute the one response God requires: "Whoever believes in Him shall not perish."

GOD GRANTS REPENTANCE

There is a beautiful truth about repentance that we must not miss: repentance itself is a gift from God.

When the early church heard that Gentiles had come to faith, they said:

> *"Well then, God has granted to the Gentiles also the repentance that leads to life."* (Acts 11:18)

Paul instructed Timothy:

> *"The Lord's bond-servant must not be quarrelsome, but be kind to all, able to teach, patient when wronged, with gentleness correcting those who are in opposition, if perhaps God may grant them repentance leading to the knowledge of the truth."* (2 Tim 2:24–26)

God "grants" repentance. He "leads" us to repentance. This is grace. We do not muster up repentance by our own willpower; God works in our hearts to bring us to the place of turning. Even the desire to repent is a gift from him.

Paul wrote:

> *"Or do you think lightly of the riches of His kindness and tolerance and patience, not knowing that the kindness of God leads you to repentance?"* (Rom 2:4)

It is God's *kindness* that leads to repentance—not his harshness, not our fear of hell, but his tender mercy and patient love. When you see how good God is, when you understand how patient he has been with you, when you grasp the love that sent Christ to the cross—*that* is what breaks your heart and draws you to repent.

If you feel drawn to repent today, that is evidence of God's grace at work in your heart. Do not resist him. Do not delay. Respond to his kindness while you can.

THE CALL TO REPENT

God commands all people everywhere to repent.

> *"Therefore having overlooked the times of ignorance, God is now declaring to men that all people everywhere should repent, because He has fixed a day in which He will judge the world in righteousness through a Man whom He has appointed, having furnished proof to all men by raising Him from the dead."* (Acts 17:30–31)

This is not a suggestion. It is a command. God "is now declaring" that "all people everywhere should repent." The resurrection of Jesus has changed everything. Judgment is certain. Repentance is urgent.

Jesus himself issued the call:

> *"I tell you, no, but unless you repent, you will all likewise perish."* (Luke 13:3)

"Unless you repent, you will perish." This is the solemn warning of Scripture. But alongside the warning stands the glorious promise:

> *"If we confess our sins, He is faithful and righteous to forgive us our sins and to cleanse us from all unrighteousness."* (1 John 1:9)

God is faithful. God is righteous. When you come to him in repentance and faith, he *will* forgive. He *will* cleanse. Not because you deserve it, but because Christ has paid for it and God keeps his promises.

Will you repent? Will you turn from your sin and turn to Christ? The prodigal's father is watching for you. He will see you coming. He will run to meet you. He will embrace you and welcome you home.

"Repent and believe in the gospel."

QUESTIONS FOR REFLECTION

- What is the difference between regret and repentance? Have you experienced true repentance?
- Why are faith and repentance inseparable? Can you have one without the other?
- Which biblical example of repentance speaks most powerfully to you? Why?
- What "fruit of repentance" should be evident in a person who has truly turned to Christ?

- Is there any sin in your life from which you need to repent today?

A PRAYER

Father, I come to You as the prodigal came home—not because I deserve to be received, but because I have nowhere else to go. I confess that I have sinned against heaven and against You. I have gone my own way. I have rebelled against Your authority. I have loved my sin more than I have loved You. I am not worthy to be called Your child. But I hear that You are merciful, that You run to meet repentant sinners, that You welcome them with joy. So I turn from my sin today. I renounce it. I hate what it has done to me and what it has cost You. And I turn to You, through Jesus Christ Your Son. Forgive me. Cleanse me. Receive me. Not because of anything I have done or will do, but because of what Christ has done for me on the cross. I believe in Him. I trust in Him. I come to Him. Thank You that Your kindness has led me to this moment. Thank You that even my desire to repent is Your gift. Hold me fast and never let me go.

Amen.

PART FOUR

THE DESTINY GOD OFFERS

". . . shall not perish, but have eternal life."

—John 3:16d

10

" . . . Shall Not Perish . . . "

The Judgment We Deserve

"It is appointed for men to die once and after this comes judgment."

—Hebrews 9:27

THE WORD WE AVOID

John 3:16 contains some of the most beautiful words in all of Scripture: God loved, God gave, whoever believes, eternal life. But nestled in the heart of this beloved verse is a word we would rather not think about: *perish.*

"Shall not perish." The promise is glorious—but it assumes a danger. If there were no peril, there would be no need for rescue. If there were no perishing, there would be no need for salvation. The good news of the gospel presupposes the bad news of judgment.

Modern culture avoids this word. We prefer to speak of God's love without mentioning his justice. We celebrate his grace while ignoring his holiness. We preach heaven but refuse to mention hell. But this is not the gospel Jesus preached. And it is not the message that will truly help anyone.

A doctor who diagnoses cancer but refuses to tell the patient is not being kind—he is being cruel. A lifeguard who sees someone drowning but doesn't want to alarm them is not being sensitive—he is being negligent. And a preacher who proclaims God's love without warning of God's judgment is not being compassionate—he is withholding the very truth that makes the gospel good news.

We must face the reality of perishing if we are to understand the wonder of not perishing.

WHAT DOES IT MEAN TO PERISH?

The Greek word translated "perish" is *apollumi* (ἀπόλλυμι). It does not mean to cease to exist. It means to be ruined, to be destroyed, to suffer loss of everything that makes existence worthwhile. It describes a state of utter ruin—existence without life, survival without hope, being without blessing.[1]

Jesus used this same word when he spoke of judgment:

> *"Do not fear those who kill the body but are unable to kill the soul; but rather fear Him who is able to destroy both soul and body in hell."* (Matt 10:28)

"Destroy" here is the same word—*apollumi*. God is able to destroy both soul and body in hell. This is not annihilation; it is devastation. It is the ruin of the whole person in the place of judgment.

John uses "perish" in contrast to "eternal life." Those who believe have eternal life; those who do not believe perish. The contrast is not between existence and non-existence but between two eternal destinies—one of blessing, one of ruin.

JESUS SPOKE OF HELL

No one in the Bible spoke more about hell than Jesus. The very one who came to save us from it warned most solemnly about its reality.

1. The Greek verb apollumi (ἀπόλλυμι) means "to destroy, ruin, or lose utterly." It does not mean annihilation but ruination—existence without life, being without blessing.

Jesus spoke of hell as a place of fire:

> *"If your hand causes you to stumble, cut it off; it is better for you to enter life crippled, than, having your two hands, to go into hell, into the unquenchable fire."* (Mark 9:43)
> *"The Son of Man will send forth His angels, and they will gather out of His kingdom all stumbling blocks, and those who commit lawlessness, and will throw them into the furnace of fire; in that place there will be weeping and gnashing of teeth."* (Matt 13:41–42)

Jesus spoke of hell as a place of darkness:

> *"But the sons of the kingdom will be cast out into the outer darkness; in that place there will be weeping and gnashing of teeth."* (Matt 8:12)

Jesus spoke of hell as a place of eternal punishment:

> *"These will go away into eternal punishment, but the righteous into eternal life."* (Matt 25:46)

Note the parallel: "eternal punishment" and "eternal life" are set side by side. If eternal life means life without end, then eternal punishment means punishment without end. The same word (*aiōnios*, αἰώνιος) describes both.

Jesus told the story of the rich man and Lazarus, in which the rich man found himself in torment after death:

> *"In Hades he lifted up his eyes, being in torment, and saw Abraham far away and Lazarus in his bosom. And he cried out and said, 'Father Abraham, have mercy on me, and send Lazarus so that he may dip the tip of his finger in water and cool off my tongue, for I am in agony in this flame.'"* (Luke 16:23–24)

Whether this story is parable or historical account, Jesus clearly taught that conscious torment awaits the unrepentant after death. This is not a metaphor that means nothing; it is a warning that means everything.

THE TESTIMONY OF SCRIPTURE

The rest of Scripture confirms what Jesus taught. Judgment is a consistent theme from Genesis to Revelation.

Paul wrote of the coming wrath:

> *"But because of your stubbornness and unrepentant heart you are storing up wrath for yourself in the day of wrath and revelation of the righteous judgment of God, who will render to each person according to his deeds."* (Rom 2:5)
> *"These will pay the penalty of eternal destruction, away from the presence of the Lord and from the glory of His power."* (2 Thess 1:9)

The writer of Hebrews declared:

> *"And inasmuch as it is appointed for men to die once and after this comes judgment."* (Heb 9:27)

> *"It is a terrifying thing to fall into the hands of the living God."* (Heb 10:31)

Peter warned:

> *"The Lord knows how to rescue the godly from temptation, and to keep the unrighteous under punishment for the day of judgment."* (2 Pet 2:9)

Jude spoke of "the punishment of eternal fire" and of those "for whom the black darkness has been reserved forever."

The book of Revelation describes the final judgment:

> *"Then I saw a great white throne and Him who sat upon it, from whose presence earth and heaven fled away, and no place was found for them. And I saw the dead, the great and the small, standing before the throne, and books were opened; and another book was opened, which is the book of life; and the dead were judged from the things which were written in the books, according to their deeds."* (Rev 20:11–12)

> *"And if anyone's name was not found written in the book of life, he was thrown into the lake of fire."* (Rev 20:15)

This is called "the second death"—not cessation of existence, but eternal separation from God and all that is good.

WHY JUDGMENT IS JUST

Many people object to the doctrine of hell. "How could a loving God send anyone to hell?" they ask. "It seems disproportionate. It seems unfair."

But this objection misunderstands several crucial realities.

We Have Sinned Against an Infinite God

The seriousness of an offense is measured not only by the act itself but by the one offended. To insult a stranger is wrong; to insult your mother is worse; to insult the king is treason. Our sins are committed against the infinitely holy, infinitely glorious, infinitely worthy God of the universe. The magnitude of the offense corresponds to the magnitude of the One offended.

We have not merely broken rules; we have rebelled against our Creator. We have not merely made mistakes; we have defied the Lord of glory. We have taken the good gifts of God and used them against him. We have suppressed the truth in unrighteousness. We have exchanged the glory of the immortal God for images and idols.

We Have Rejected Infinite Grace

God has not left us without witness. He has revealed himself in creation. He has written his law on our hearts. He has sent prophets and apostles. Most of all, he has sent his own Son. To reject all of this—to turn away from such persistent, patient, costly love—is not a small thing.

Jesus wept over Jerusalem because they rejected him:

> *"Jerusalem, Jerusalem, who kills the prophets and stones those who are sent to her! How often I wanted to gather*

> *your children together, the way a hen gathers her chicks under her wings, and you were unwilling."* (Matt 23:37)

"You were unwilling." Hell is not God's arbitrary sentence; it is the destination chosen by those who refuse his grace. As C. S. Lewis wrote: "The doors of hell are locked on the inside." Those who perish have rejected the only remedy for their condition.[2]

God Must Be Just

If God simply overlooked sin, he would not be just. If he let the wicked go unpunished, he would be complicit in their wickedness. A judge who ignores crime is a corrupt judge. A God who ignores sin would be an unjust God.

> *"The LORD is slow to anger and great in power, and the LORD will by no means leave the guilty unpunished."* (Nah 1:3)

God's justice is not a flaw in his character; it is the foundation of his throne. Heaven and earth depend on his righteousness. If he were to let sin slide, the moral fabric of the universe would unravel.

The question is not "How could a loving God send anyone to hell?" The question is "How could a holy God let anyone into heaven?" That he has made a way—through the sacrifice of his Son—is the marvel of the gospel.

THE HORROR OF SEPARATION FROM GOD

Perhaps the most terrible aspect of perishing is eternal separation from God. Paul described it as being "away from the presence of the Lord and from the glory of His power."

Every good thing in this life comes from God. Every moment of joy, every experience of beauty, every relationship of love, every

2. C. S. Lewis, The Great Divorce (New York: HarperOne, 2001), 72. Originally published 1945; see also The Problem of Pain (New York: HarperOne, 2001), 130–131 for Lewis's related argument about the self-chosen nature of hell.

taste of pleasure—all of it is a gift from the Father of lights, "with whom there is no variation or shifting shadow." Even those who do not acknowledge God enjoy his blessings daily.

But what if all of that were removed? What if you were cut off from every vestige of God's goodness? No love, because God is love. No light, because God is light. No joy, no peace, no hope, no comfort—because all of these flow from God's presence.

This is the outer darkness. This is the place of weeping and gnashing of teeth. Not merely punishment inflicted from outside, but the natural consequence of being separated from the source of all good.

Hell is getting what we ask for. If we spend our lives saying to God, "Leave me alone; I want nothing to do with you; I will be my own god"—then eventually God says, "Very well." And that is hell.

The cry of the lost will be the most agonizing words ever spoken: "Depart from Me." Those are the words Jesus will speak to the unrepentant at the final judgment:

> *"Then He will also say to those on His left, 'Depart from Me, accursed ones, into the eternal fire which has been prepared for the devil and his angels.'"* (Matt 25:41)

"Depart from Me." These are words of final, irreversible separation. The door closes. The opportunity ends. The judgment is sealed forever.

ALL HAVE SINNED

But why does this apply to me? Why am I in danger of perishing?

The answer is painfully simple: because you have sinned.

> *"For all have sinned and fall short of the glory of God."* (Rom 3:23)

> *"There is none righteous, not even one; there is none who understands, there is none who seeks for God; all have turned aside, together they have become useless; there is none who does good, there is not even one."* (Rom 3:10–12)

"All have sinned." "There is none righteous." "Not even one." This is the universal verdict of Scripture. No one is exempt. No one is excused. From the greatest saint to the worst criminal, all stand guilty before God.

You may not consider yourself a great sinner. You may have lived a relatively moral life. You may compare favorably to others around you. But the standard is not other people—the standard is God's perfect holiness.

> *"For whoever keeps the whole law and yet stumbles in one point, he has become guilty of all."* (Jas 2:10)

One sin is enough to condemn. One lie. One lustful thought. One moment of pride. One act of selfishness. The law is like a chain—break one link, and the whole chain is broken. You cannot be mostly innocent before a holy God.

> *"For the wages of sin is death."* (Rom 6:23)

The wages of sin—what sin earns, what sin deserves—is death. Not merely physical death, but spiritual death: eternal separation from God. This is what we have earned. This is what we deserve. This is the destiny toward which we are all heading apart from God's intervention.

THE GOOD NEWS: "SHALL NOT PERISH"

But here is the glory of the gospel. Here is the wonder of John 3:16. Here is the good news that changes everything:

> "*. . . that whoever believes in Him shall not perish . . .* " (John 3:16)

"Shall *not* perish." This is not a vague hope. It is not wishful thinking. It is a promise—a divine guarantee from the lips of Jesus himself. Whoever believes in him *shall not perish.*

The judgment we deserve will not fall on us. The wrath we have earned will not consume us. The perishing we are headed toward will not be our destiny. Why? Because it fell on Christ instead.

> *"He Himself bore our sins in His body on the cross."* (1 Pet 2:24)
>
> *"Christ redeemed us from the curse of the Law, having become a curse for us."* (Gal 3:13)
>
> *"He made Him who knew no sin to be sin on our behalf, so that we might become the righteousness of God in Him."* (2 Cor 5:21)

On the cross, Jesus experienced the perishing that we deserved. He was forsaken so that we might be accepted. He was condemned so that we might be acquitted. He drank the cup of God's wrath so that we might drink the cup of salvation.

> *"Therefore there is now no condemnation for those who are in Christ Jesus."* (Rom 8:1)

"No condemnation." None. Zero. The verdict has been rendered. The case is closed. If you are in Christ Jesus—if you have believed in him—there is no judgment waiting for you. Your sins have been paid for. Your record has been cleared. You shall not perish.

Paul exulted in this truth:

> *"Who will bring a charge against God's elect? God is the one who justifies; who is the one who condemns? Christ Jesus is He who died, yes, rather who was raised, who is at the right hand of God, who also intercedes for us."* (Rom 8:33–34)

Who will bring a charge? No one. Who will condemn? No one. The Judge himself has declared you righteous. The Son himself stands at his right hand, interceding for you. You are secure. You are safe. You shall not perish.

THE URGENCY OF THE MESSAGE

If all of this is true—if perishing is real, if judgment is coming, if hell awaits the unrepentant—then the message of the gospel is more urgent than we have imagined.

This is not a matter of religious preference. It is not about choosing a spiritual path that suits your personality. It is about rescue from ruin. It is about salvation from destruction. It is about escaping the wrath to come.

> *"How will we escape if we neglect so great a salvation?"* (Heb 2:3)

There is no escape for those who neglect. There is no second chance after death. There is no other name by which we must be saved.

But for those who believe—for whoever believes—there is complete deliverance. The promise stands: you shall not perish.

Do you believe? Have you trusted in Christ? Are you sure—not because of your own goodness, but because of his sacrifice—that you will not perish?

If not, today is the day to believe. Today is the day to flee from the wrath to come. Today is the day to take shelter in Christ.

> *"Behold, now is 'the acceptable time,' behold, now is 'the day of salvation.'"* (2 Cor 6:2)

QUESTIONS FOR REFLECTION

- Why do you think modern culture avoids talking about hell and judgment? What are the consequences of this silence?
- How does understanding the reality of perishing deepen your appreciation for the gospel?
- Why is it just for God to punish sin eternally? How would you answer someone who says this is unfair?
- What does it mean that "the doors of hell are locked on the inside"?
- Are you certain that you "shall not perish"? On what basis does your confidence rest?

A PRAYER

Holy God, I confess that I have sinned against You. I have rebelled against Your authority. I have broken Your law. I have lived as if You did not exist, as if my choices had no consequences, as if I would never stand before Your judgment seat. I see now that I am in danger—real, eternal danger. I deserve to perish. I deserve Your wrath. I have no defense, no excuse, no merit of my own. But I hear that You have provided a way of escape. I hear that Christ bore the judgment I deserve. I hear that whoever believes in Him shall not perish. So I believe. I trust in Christ alone. I take shelter in His sacrifice. I claim His righteousness as my own. Thank You that there is now no condemnation for me. Thank You that I shall not perish. Thank You that the judgment that was coming for me fell on Jesus instead. Help me to live in the light of this great salvation—with gratitude, with urgency, with a heart that longs to see others rescued as I have been rescued.

Amen.

11

" . . . But Have Eternal Life"

The Gift Beyond Imagination

"This is eternal life, that they may know You, the only true God, and Jesus Christ whom You have sent."

—John 17:3

THE CLIMAX OF JOHN 3:16

We have come at last to the glorious conclusion of John 3:16: " . . . but have eternal life."

The verse has traced a magnificent arc. It began with God—his love for the world. It moved to the gift—his only begotten Son. It described the response—whoever believes in him. It stated the negative result—shall not perish. And now it reaches its climax with the positive promise: eternal life.

This is what God offers. This is what Christ purchased. This is what faith receives. Not merely escape from perishing—though that alone would be reason for eternal gratitude—but the gift of eternal life.

MORE THAN ENDLESS DURATION

When we hear "eternal life," we typically think of quantity—life that goes on forever. And this is certainly true. The Greek word *aiōnios* (αἰώνιος) does mean "everlasting." Those who believe will live forever.[1]

But eternal life in the Bible is not merely about duration. It is about *quality*. Jesus defined eternal life in his great prayer:

> *"This is eternal life, that they may know You, the only true God, and Jesus Christ whom You have sent."* (John 17:3)

Notice: eternal life is defined not as living forever but as *knowing God*. It is relational. It is personal. It is intimate communion with the Father and the Son.

> *"I came that they may have life, and have it abundantly."* (John 10:10)

Jesus came to give *abundant* life—life overflowing, life to the full, life as it was meant to be lived.

KNOWING GOD

If eternal life is knowing God, we must ask: What does it mean to "know" him?

In the Bible, "knowing" involves intimate, personal, experiential relationship. The same Hebrew word (*yada*) is used for the most intimate relationship between husband and wife. To know God is not merely to know *about* him; it is to know *him*—personally, deeply, progressively.

Paul expressed this as his supreme ambition:

> *"That I may know Him and the power of His resurrection and the fellowship of His sufferings."* (Phil 3:10)

God spoke through Jeremiah:

1. The Greek adjective aiōnios (αἰώνιος) refers to the "age to come" (aiōn) and describes both duration (everlasting) and quality (the life of the coming age).

> *"Let him who boasts boast of this, that he understands and knows Me."* (Jer 9:24)

The greatest treasure is not wisdom, power, or wealth. It is knowing God.

ETERNAL LIFE BEGINS NOW

Here is a truth that surprises many people: eternal life is not merely future; it is present.

> *"Truly, truly, I say to you, he who hears My word, and believes Him who sent Me, has eternal life, and does not come into judgment, but has passed out of death into life."* (John 5:24)

Notice the verb tense: "*has* eternal life." Not "will have" but "has." The moment you believe, you possess eternal life.[2]

> *"These things I have written to you who believe in the name of the Son of God, so that you may know that you have eternal life."* (1 John 5:13)

> *"Therefore if anyone is in Christ, he is a new creature; the old things passed away; behold, new things have come."* (2 Cor 5:17)

THE BLESSINGS OF ETERNAL LIFE NOW

Peace with God

> *"Therefore, having been justified by faith, we have peace with God through our Lord Jesus Christ."* (Rom 5:1)

2. The present tense "has" (echei, ἔχει) in John 3:36 indicates present possession of eternal life, not merely future hope.

Access to the Father

"For through Him we both have our access in one Spirit to the Father." (Eph 2:18)

The Indwelling Spirit

"Do you not know that you are a temple of God and that the Spirit of God dwells in you?" (1 Cor 3:16)

Joy Inexpressible

"Though you have not seen Him, you love Him, and though you do not see Him now, but believe in Him, you greatly rejoice with joy inexpressible and full of glory." (1 Pet 1:8)

Hope That Does Not Disappoint

"And hope does not disappoint, because the love of God has been poured out within our hearts through the Holy Spirit." (Rom 5:5)

THE INHERITANCE RESERVED IN HEAVEN

"Blessed be the God and Father of our Lord Jesus Christ, who according to His great mercy has caused us to be born again to a living hope through the resurrection of Jesus Christ from the dead, to obtain an inheritance which is imperishable and undefiled and will not fade away, reserved in heaven for you." (1 Pet 1:3–5)

"In My Father's house are many dwelling places; if it were not so, I would have told you; for I go to prepare a place for you." (John 14:2)

"Things which eye has not seen and ear has not heard, and which have not entered the heart of man, all that God has prepared for those who love Him." (1 Cor 2:9)

THE RESURRECTION BODY

"Who will transform the body of our humble state into conformity with the body of His glory." (Phil 3:21)

"It is sown a perishable body, it is raised an imperishable body; it is sown in dishonor, it is raised in glory; it is sown in weakness, it is raised in power." (1 Cor 15:42–43)

"For this perishable must put on the imperishable, and this mortal must put on immortality. Then will come about the saying that is written, 'Death is swallowed up in victory.'" (1 Cor 15:53–54)

THE NEW HEAVENS AND NEW EARTH

"For behold, I create new heavens and a new earth; and the former things will not be remembered or come to mind." (Isa 65:17)

"Then I saw a new heaven and a new earth . . . And I heard a loud voice from the throne, saying, 'Behold, the tabernacle of God is among men, and He will dwell among them.'" (Rev 21:1, 3)

"And He will wipe away every tear from their eyes; and there will no longer be any death; there will no longer be any mourning, or crying, or pain." (Rev 21:4)

"Behold, I am making all things new." (Rev 21:5)

SEEING GOD FACE TO FACE

> *"Blessed are the pure in heart, for they shall see God."* (Matt 5:8)
>
> *"For now we see in a mirror dimly, but then face to face; now I know in part, but then I will know fully just as I also have been fully known."* (1 Cor 13:12)
>
> *"They will see His face, and His name will be on their foreheads."* (Rev 22:4)

This is the beatific vision—the sight of God himself in all his beauty, all his majesty, all his love.

THE GIFT IS YOURS

> *"For the wages of sin is death, but the free gift of God is eternal life in Christ Jesus our Lord."* (Rom 6:23)

A free gift. Not wages earned but grace given. Will you receive it?

QUESTIONS FOR REFLECTION

- How does knowing that eternal life is about quality (knowing God) rather than just quantity (living forever) change your understanding?
- What does it mean to you that eternal life begins now, not just when you die?
- Which present blessing of eternal life is most meaningful to you right now?
- How does the promise of resurrection affect how you view suffering in this life?
- What does it mean to you that you will one day see God face to face?

A PRAYER

Father, I am overwhelmed by what You offer. Eternal life—not just endless existence, but abundant life, knowing You, dwelling with You forever. Thank You that eternal life has already begun—that I have peace with You, that Your Spirit lives within me. Thank You for the inheritance reserved in heaven, the resurrection body, the new heavens and new earth. Thank You most of all that I will see Your face. Help me to live as one who has eternal life—with hope that does not disappoint, with joy inexpressible, with love for the Savior who made it all possible.

Amen.

12

What Eternal Life Looks Like

Now and Forever

"For to me, to live is Christ and to die is gain."

—Philippians 1:21

A LIFE TRANSFORMED

We have seen that eternal life is not merely a future destination but a present possession. The moment you believe in Christ, you have eternal life. But what does this new life look like? How does eternal life express itself in the daily experience of the believer?

The answer is: everything changes. Eternal life transforms every dimension of human existence.

> *"But we all, with unveiled face, beholding as in a mirror the glory of the Lord, are being transformed into the same image from glory to glory, just as from the Lord, the Spirit."* (2 Cor 3:18)[1]

1. The Greek verb metamorphoumetha (μεταμορφούμεθα) in 2 Corinthians 3:18 is a present passive, indicating an ongoing process accomplished by God.

"Being transformed." This is sanctification—the lifelong process by which God makes us holy.

THE PROCESS OF SANCTIFICATION

When you trusted Christ, you were justified—declared righteous in God's sight. Sanctification is the gradual process by which you actually become righteous in your character and conduct.

> *"For this is the will of God, your sanctification."* (1 Thess 4:3)
>
> *"Now may the God of peace Himself sanctify you entirely; and may your spirit and soul and body be preserved complete, without blame at the coming of our Lord Jesus Christ. Faithful is He who calls you, and He also will bring it to pass."* (1 Thess 5:23)
>
> *"Work out your salvation with fear and trembling; for it is God who is at work in you, both to will and to work for His good pleasure."* (Phil 2:12–13)

"Work out your salvation . . . for it is God who is at work in you." Both are true. You must work—but the power behind your working is God himself.

PUTTING OFF AND PUTTING ON

> *"Lay aside the old self, which is being corrupted in accordance with the lusts of deceit, and be renewed in the spirit of your mind, and put on the new self, which in the likeness of God has been created in righteousness and holiness of the truth."* (Eph 4:22–24)
>
> *"But the fruit of the Spirit is love, joy, peace, patience, kindness, goodness, faithfulness, gentleness, self-control; against such things there is no law."* (Gal 5:22–23)

This is what the Holy Spirit produces in those who walk with him.

WALKING WITH GOD DAILY

Through Prayer

"Pray without ceasing." (1 Thess 5:17)

"Be anxious for nothing, but in everything by prayer and supplication with thanksgiving let your requests be made known to God. And the peace of God, which surpasses all comprehension, will guard your hearts and your minds in Christ Jesus." (Phil 4:6–7)

Through Scripture

"Your word is a lamp to my feet and a light to my path." (Ps 119:105)

"All Scripture is inspired by God and profitable for teaching, for reproof, for correction, for training in righteousness." (2 Tim 3:16)

Through Fellowship

"And let us consider how to stimulate one another to love and good deeds, not forsaking our own assembling together, as is the habit of some, but encouraging one another." (Heb 10:24–25)

Through Service

"For we are His workmanship, created in Christ Jesus for good works, which God prepared beforehand so that we would walk in them." (Eph 2:10)

THE BELIEVER'S HOPE IN DEATH

For the believer, death is not the end; it is a doorway.

> *"For to me, to live is Christ and to die is gain."* (Phil 1:21)
>
> *"Having the desire to depart and be with Christ, for that is very much better."* (Phil 1:23)
>
> *"O death, where is your victory? O death, where is your sting? The sting of death is sin, and the power of sin is the law; but thanks be to God, who gives us the victory through our Lord Jesus Christ."* (1 Cor 15:55–57)

ABSENT FROM THE BODY, PRESENT WITH THE LORD

> *"We are of good courage, I say, and prefer rather to be absent from the body and to be at home with the Lord."* (2 Cor 5:8)
>
> *"Truly I say to you, today you shall be with Me in Paradise."* (Luke 23:43)

"Today." The moment the believer's body dies, the believer's spirit is at home with Christ.

WHAT HEAVEN WILL BE LIKE

The Presence of God

> *"They will see His face, and His name will be on their foreheads. And there will no longer be any night; and they will not have need of the light of a lamp nor the light of the sun, because the Lord God will illumine them; and they will reign forever and ever."* (Rev 22:4–5)

Perfect Worship

"Worthy is the Lamb that was slain to receive power and riches and wisdom and might and honor and glory and blessing." (Rev 5:12)

Perfect Fellowship

"After these things I looked, and behold, a great multitude which no one could count, from every nation and all tribes and peoples and tongues, standing before the throne and before the Lamb." (Rev 7:9)

No More Sorrow

"He will wipe away every tear from their eyes; and there will no longer be any death; there will no longer be any mourning, or crying, or pain; the first things have passed away." (Rev 21:4)

LIVING IN LIGHT OF ETERNITY

"If you have been raised up with Christ, keep seeking the things above, where Christ is, seated at the right hand of God. Set your mind on the things above, not on the things that are on earth." (Col 3:1–2)

"For momentary, light affliction is producing for us an eternal weight of glory far beyond all comparison, while we look not at the things which are seen, but at the things which are not seen; for the things which are seen are temporal, but the things which are not seen are eternal." (2 Cor 4:17–18)

"Therefore, my beloved brethren, be steadfast, immovable, always abounding in the work of the Lord, knowing that your toil is not in vain in the Lord." (1 Cor 15:58)

C. S. Lewis wrote: "If you read history you will find that the Christians who did most for the present world were just those who thought most of the next."[2]

THE HOPE THAT DOES NOT DISAPPOINT

> *"And this is the promise which He Himself made to us: eternal life."* (1 John 2:25)
>
> *"He who testifies to these things says, 'Yes, I am coming quickly.' Amen. Come, Lord Jesus."* (Rev 22:20)

QUESTIONS FOR REFLECTION

- What evidence of transformation do you see in your life since you came to faith in Christ?
- Which of the spiritual disciplines (prayer, Scripture, fellowship, service) do you most need to strengthen?
- How does the Christian view of death differ from the world's view?
- Which aspect of heaven are you most looking forward to?
- How would your daily life change if you truly lived "in light of eternity"?

A PRAYER

Father, thank You for the gift of eternal life. Continue Your work in me. Sanctify me entirely. Make me more like Jesus. Give me discipline to pray, to read Your Word, to gather with Your people, to serve in Your name. Give me a living hope for what is to come. Help me

2. C. S. Lewis, Mere Christianity (New York: HarperOne, 2001), 134.

to face death without fear. Fix my eyes on the things above. Keep me faithful until that day. Amen.

PART FIVE

THE DECISION BEFORE YOU

"Whoever believes in Him shall not perish,
but have eternal life."

—John 3:16

13

Counting the Cost

What Following Jesus Requires

"If anyone wishes to come after Me, he must deny himself, and take up his cross and follow Me."

—Matthew 16:24

A DIFFERENT KIND OF INVITATION

We have explored the magnificent offer of John 3:16: eternal life as a free gift to whoever believes. Salvation is by grace alone, through faith alone, in Christ alone.

But we must not misunderstand this gift. While salvation is free, it is not cheap. While eternal life cannot be earned, it does demand everything.

> *"Now large crowds were going along with Him; and He turned and said to them, 'If anyone comes to Me, and does not hate his own father and mother and wife and children and brothers and sisters, yes, and even his own life, he cannot be My disciple. Whoever does not carry his own cross and come after Me cannot be My disciple.'"* (Luke 14:25–26)

Jesus wants followers, not fans. He seeks disciples, not admirers.

COUNT THE COST

> *"For which one of you, when he wants to build a tower, does not first sit down and calculate the cost to see if he has enough to complete it?"* (Luke 14:28)
>
> *"Or what king, when he sets out to meet another king in battle, will not first sit down and consider whether he is strong enough with ten thousand men to encounter the one coming against him with twenty thousand?"* (Luke 14:31)
>
> *"So then, none of you can be My disciple who does not give up all his own possessions."* (Luke 14:33)

This does not mean every Christian must take a vow of poverty. It means everything must be surrendered to his lordship.

DENY YOURSELF

> *"If anyone wishes to come after Me, he must deny himself, and take up his cross and follow Me."* (Matt 16:24)

"Deny himself." This means renouncing your right to run your own life—dethroning yourself and enthroning Christ.

> *"I have been crucified with Christ; and it is no longer I who live, but Christ lives in me."* (Gal 2:20)
>
> *"For whoever wishes to save his life will lose it; but whoever loses his life for My sake will find it."* (Matt 16:25)

TAKE UP YOUR CROSS

> *"If anyone wishes to come after Me, he must deny himself, and take up his cross daily and follow Me."* (Luke 9:23)

Note the word "daily." This is not a one-time decision but a daily practice.

FOLLOW ME

"A disciple is not above his teacher, nor a slave above his master. It is enough for the disciple that he become like his teacher." (Matt 10:24–25)

"My sheep hear My voice, and I know them, and they follow Me; and I give eternal life to them, and they will never perish." (John 10:27–28)

THE COST OF DISCIPLESHIP

It May Cost Your Relationships

"Do not think that I came to bring peace on the earth; I did not come to bring peace, but a sword. For I came to set a man against his father, and a daughter against her mother." (Matt 10:34–35)

It May Cost Your Reputation

"Blessed are you when people insult you and persecute you, and falsely say all kinds of evil against you because of Me." (Matt 5:11)

It May Cost Your Comfort

"The foxes have holes and the birds of the air have nests, but the Son of Man has nowhere to lay His head." (Matt 8:20)

It May Cost Your Life

> *"Do not fear those who kill the body but are unable to kill the soul."* (Matt 10:28)
>
> *"They overcame him because of the blood of the Lamb and because of the word of their testimony, and they did not love their life even when faced with death."* (Rev 12:11)

THE COST OF NON-DISCIPLESHIP

What does it cost to refuse Christ?

> *"For what will it profit a man if he gains the whole world and forfeits his soul?"* (Matt 16:26)

Dietrich Bonhoeffer wrote: "When Christ calls a man, he bids him come and die." But the alternative to discipleship is not a life of ease—it is a life of loss.[1]

JESUS IS WORTH EVERYTHING

> *"The kingdom of heaven is like a treasure hidden in the field, which a man found and hid again; and from joy over it he goes and sells all that he has and buys that field."* (Matt 13:44)

Notice: the man sold everything "from joy." Jesus is that valuable.

> *"But whatever things were gain to me, those things I have counted as loss for the sake of Christ. More than that, I count all things to be loss in view of the surpassing value of knowing Christ Jesus my Lord."* (Phil 3:7–8)

1. Dietrich Bonhoeffer, The Cost of Discipleship, trans. R. H. Fuller (New York: Touchstone, 1995), 89. Originally published as Nachfolge (Munich: Chr. Kaiser Verlag, 1937).

FOLLOWING JESUS IN A HOSTILE WORLD

> *"If the world hates you, you know that it has hated Me before it hated you."* (John 15:18)
>
> *"Indeed, all who desire to live godly in Christ Jesus will be persecuted."* (2 Tim 3:12)
>
> *"These things I have spoken to you, so that in Me you may have peace. In the world you have tribulation, but take courage; I have overcome the world."* (John 16:33)

THE INVITATION STANDS

> *"Come to Me, all who are weary and heavy-laden, and I will give you rest. Take My yoke upon you and learn from Me, for I am gentle and humble in heart, and you will find rest for your souls. For My yoke is easy and My burden is light."* (Matt 11:28–29)

His yoke is easy. His burden is light. Not because discipleship costs nothing, but because he bears the weight with us.

Will you follow him?

QUESTIONS FOR REFLECTION

- What does it mean to you personally to "deny yourself" and "take up your cross"?
- What has following Jesus cost you? What might it cost you in the future?
- Why do you think Jesus warned people to count the cost before following him?
- How does the "cost of non-discipleship" compare to the cost of discipleship?
- Is Jesus worth everything to you? How does your life reflect your answer?

A PRAYER

Lord Jesus, I have heard Your call. I have counted the cost. And I have seen that You are worth infinitely more than anything I could give up. I deny myself—I renounce my right to run my own life. I take up my cross—I accept whatever suffering may come from following You. I will follow You—wherever You lead, whatever it costs, for as long as I live. Give me strength to follow when it is hard. Give me courage to stand when the world opposes me. You are the treasure worth selling everything to possess. Amen.

14

Common Obstacles

Answering the Objections

"Come now, and let us reason together," says the LORD.

—Isaiah 1:18

OBSTACLES ON THE PATH

The invitation of John 3:16 is clear: "Whoever believes in Him shall not perish, but have eternal life." But many people find themselves hesitating. They have heard the gospel, they may even be drawn to it, but something holds them back.

These obstacles are real. They deserve honest answers. God does not ask us to believe blindly. He invites us to reason with him.

"I'M NOT GOOD ENOUGH"

This is perhaps the most common obstacle. "God could never accept someone like me."

If this is your objection, I have good news: You're right. You're not good enough. Neither am I. Neither is anyone.

> *"For all have sinned and fall short of the glory of God."* (Rom 3:23)

The gospel is not for good people. It is for sinners.

> *"It is not those who are healthy who need a physician, but those who are sick; I did not come to call the righteous, but sinners."* (Mark 2:17)
>
> *"Christ Jesus came into the world to save sinners, among whom I am foremost of all. Yet for this reason I found mercy, so that in me as the foremost, Jesus Christ might demonstrate His perfect patience as an example for those who would believe in Him for eternal life."* (1 Tim 1:15–16)

If Jesus saved Paul—a man who had persecuted Christians—then no one is beyond his reach.

"I'LL DO IT LATER"

"I want to enjoy life first. I'll think about God when I'm older."

The problem is that you are not promised tomorrow.

> *"Do not boast about tomorrow, for you do not know what a day may bring forth."* (Prov 27:1)
>
> *"You are just a vapor that appears for a little while and then vanishes away."* (Jas 4:14)
>
> *"God said to him, 'You fool! This very night your soul is required of you.'"* (Luke 12:20)
>
> *"Today if you hear His voice, do not harden your hearts."* (Heb 3:15)
>
> *"Behold, now is 'the acceptable time,' behold, now is 'the day of salvation.'"* (2 Cor 6:2)

"I HAVE TOO MANY QUESTIONS"

"I can't believe because I have too many unanswered questions."

> *"You will seek Me and find Me when you search for Me with all your heart."* (Jer 29:13)

You will never have all your questions answered before you believe. Faith is not the absence of doubt; it is trust in the midst of uncertainty.

> *"I do believe; help my unbelief."* (Mark 9:24)

You can come to Christ with imperfect faith. You can come with lingering questions. Just come.

"WHAT ABOUT OTHER RELIGIONS?"

"How can you say Jesus is the only way?"

> *"Jesus said to him, 'I am the way, and the truth, and the life; no one comes to the Father but through Me.'"* (John 14:6)

> *"And there is salvation in no one else; for there is no other name under heaven that has been given among men by which we must be saved."* (Acts 4:12)

These are exclusive claims. But if Jesus really is who he claimed to be, then it is not arrogant to say he is the only way. It is simply true.

"I TRIED CHRISTIANITY AND IT DIDN'T WORK"

What exactly did you try? Did you try religion or relationship?

> *"Not everyone who says to Me, 'Lord, Lord,' will enter the kingdom of heaven, but he who does the will of My Father who is in heaven. Many will say to Me on that day, 'Lord, Lord, did we not prophesy in Your name?' And then I will declare to them, 'I never knew you.'"* (Matt 7:21–23)

> *"They went out from us, but they were not really of us; for if they had been of us, they would have remained with us."* (1 John 2:19)

Perhaps you never really knew Christ, only religion. Christ is not a program that didn't work; he is a Person who loves you still.

"CHRISTIANS ARE HYPOCRITES"

If you have been wounded by people who claimed to follow Christ, I am sorry. The church has often failed to represent Jesus well.

But the failures of Christians do not disprove Christ. The question is: Who is Jesus?

> *"He committed no sin, nor was any deceit found in His mouth; and while being reviled, He did not revile in return."* (1 Pet 2:22)

Jesus is not a hypocrite. He practiced what he preached perfectly. Do not let the failures of people keep you from the faithfulness of Christ.

"I'M AFRAID OF WHAT I'LL HAVE TO GIVE UP"

Following Jesus does require change. But consider what you are being asked to give up: sin. And sin is what destroys you.

> *"Everyone who commits sin is the slave of sin . . . So if the Son makes you free, you will be free indeed."* (John 8:34, 36)

> *"The thief comes only to steal and kill and destroy; I came that they may have life, and have it abundantly."* (John 10:10)

THE REAL OBSTACLE

Beneath all objections lies one fundamental obstacle: the human will.

> *"This is the judgment, that the Light has come into the world, and men loved the darkness rather than the Light, for their deeds were evil."* (John 3:19)

> *"But he who practices the truth comes to the Light, so that his deeds may be manifested as having been wrought in God."* (John 3:21)

The question is not whether you have objections but whether you are willing to let those objections be answered.

QUESTIONS FOR REFLECTION

- Which of the obstacles discussed in this chapter have you personally struggled with?
- Why is "I'm not good enough" actually the right starting point for understanding the gospel?
- What is the danger of saying "I'll do it later"?
- How would you respond to someone who says, "I can't believe because I have too many questions"?
- What might be the "real obstacle" beneath your intellectual objections?

A PRAYER

Lord, I confess that I have hidden behind excuses. I have used questions as shields and objections as walls. But I am tired of hiding. I want to come into the light. I know I am not good enough—but I believe Jesus is. I know I should not delay—so I am coming now. I still have questions—but I choose to trust You in the midst of them. Forgive my excuses. Overcome my resistance. I believe; help my unbelief. Amen.

15

Today Is the Day

The Urgency of Belief

"Behold, now is 'the acceptable time,' behold, now is 'the day of salvation.'"

—2 CORINTHIANS 6:2

THE MOMENT OF DECISION

We have come to the end of our journey through John 3:16. We have explored every word, every phrase, every promise. We have seen the God who loves, the gift he gave, the response he requires, and the destiny he offers.

Now there is only one thing left: your decision.

"Whoever believes in Him shall not perish, but have eternal life."

This promise has stood for two thousand years. It has been embraced by billions of people across every nation, every culture, every century. Kings and peasants, scholars and children, the morally upright and the utterly broken—all have found in this verse the answer to their deepest need.

The question now is: Will you believe?

THE URGENCY OF TODAY

> *"Behold, now is 'the acceptable time,' behold, now is 'the day of salvation.'"* (2 Cor 6:2)

Not tomorrow. Not next week. Not when you've sorted out your life. *Now*. Today.

Why is today so urgent?

Because Tomorrow Is Not Promised

> *"Come now, you who say, 'Today or tomorrow we will go to such and such a city, and spend a year there and engage in business and make a profit.' Yet you do not know what your life will be like tomorrow. You are just a vapor that appears for a little while and then vanishes away."* (Jas 4:13–14)

Life is fragile. It is a vapor, a mist, a breath. Here today, gone tomorrow. You have no guarantee of another hour, another day, another year.

Because Hearts Grow Hard

> *"Today if you hear His voice, do not harden your hearts."* (Heb 3:15)

Every time you hear the gospel and say "not yet," your heart becomes a little harder. Every delay makes the next decision more difficult. The voice that seems clear today may grow faint tomorrow.

Because Judgment Is Certain

> *"And inasmuch as it is appointed for men to die once and after this comes judgment."* (Heb 9:27)

Death is not the end—it is the doorway to judgment. And after death, there are no second chances. The rich man in torment could not cross the great chasm that separated him from Abraham. The door, once closed, stays closed.

WHAT YOU MUST BELIEVE

What does it mean to believe in Jesus? We have explored this at length, but let me summarize:

Believe that you are a sinner. "For all have sinned and fall short of the glory of God." You cannot be saved until you know you are lost. You cannot receive a Savior until you know you need one.

Believe that Jesus is the Son of God. "These are written so that you may believe that Jesus is the Christ, the Son of God." He is not merely a teacher, a prophet, or a good man. He is God in human flesh, come to save you.

Believe that Jesus died for your sins. "Christ died for our sins according to the Scriptures." He bore the punishment you deserved. He paid the debt you could not pay.

Believe that Jesus rose from the dead. "If you confess with your mouth Jesus as Lord, and believe in your heart that God raised Him from the dead, you will be saved." The resurrection is God's seal of approval on everything Jesus claimed and accomplished.

Believe that Jesus alone can save you. "And there is salvation in no one else." Not your good works, not your religious rituals, not your sincere efforts—Jesus alone.

HOW TO RESPOND

If you have understood the message of this book and want to receive eternal life, here is how to respond:

Acknowledge Your Need

Come to God honestly. Admit that you are a sinner. Stop making excuses. Stop comparing yourself to others. Agree with God's verdict on your life: "I have sinned against You."

Turn from Your Sin

Repentance is not merely feeling sorry; it is turning around. It is abandoning your old way of life and embracing God's way. You cannot cling to your sin and cling to Christ at the same time.

Trust in Jesus

Saving faith is not merely believing facts about Jesus. It is personal trust in Jesus himself. It is receiving him, resting in him, relying on him alone for salvation.

> *"But as many as received Him, to them He gave the right to become children of God, even to those who believe in His name."* (John 1:12)

Confess Him as Lord

> *"If you confess with your mouth Jesus as Lord, and believe in your heart that God raised Him from the dead, you will be saved; for with the heart a person believes, resulting in righteousness, and with the mouth he confesses, resulting in salvation."* (Rom 10:9–10)

To confess Jesus as Lord is to acknowledge his authority over your life. He is no longer just Savior but Master—the one you will follow and obey.

A PRAYER OF FAITH

If you are ready to believe, you may wish to express your faith in a prayer like this:

Lord Jesus Christ, I come to You today. I confess that I am a sinner. I have lived my life apart from You. I have broken Your laws. I have gone my own way. I deserve Your judgment.

But I believe that You are the Son of God. I believe that You died on the cross for my sins. I believe that You rose from the dead. I believe that You are able to save me—and I ask You to save me now.

I turn from my sin. I turn to You. I receive You as my Savior. I confess You as my Lord. I trust You completely—not my own works, not my own goodness, but You alone.

Thank You for loving me. Thank You for dying for me. Thank You for the gift of eternal life. I receive it now by faith. I am Yours forever.

In Jesus' name, Amen.

WHAT HAPPENS NOW?

If you have sincerely believed in Jesus, several things are now true of you:

You Are Forgiven

> *"In Him we have redemption through His blood, the forgiveness of our trespasses, according to the riches of His grace."* (Eph 1:7)

Every sin—past, present, and future—has been paid for by Christ. Your record has been wiped clean.

You Are a Child of God

> *"But as many as received Him, to them He gave the right to become children of God."* (John 1:12)

You are no longer a stranger, an enemy, an outsider. You are a child of the King, adopted into his family forever.

You Have Eternal Life

> *"He who believes in the Son has eternal life."* (John 3:36)

Not "will have" but "has." Right now. The moment you believed, eternal life became yours.

You Are Secure

> *"I give eternal life to them, and they will never perish; and no one will snatch them out of My hand."* (John 10:28)

You did not save yourself, and you cannot unsave yourself. You are held by Christ and held by the Father. No one can snatch you away.

WHAT TO DO NEXT

Your new life in Christ has just begun. Here are your next steps:

Tell someone. Share your decision with a Christian friend, a pastor, or a family member. Confession is part of faith.

Be baptized. Baptism is the public declaration of your faith—the outward sign of the inward change.[1]

1. The Greek verb baptizō (βαπτίζω) means "to dip, immerse, or submerge." See G. R. Beasley-Murray, Baptism in the New Testament (Grand Rapids: Eerdmans, 1962).

Join a church. You were not meant to follow Christ alone. Find a Bible-believing church where you can grow, serve, and be encouraged.

Read the Bible. Start with the Gospel of John, which tells the story of Jesus. Then continue through the New Testament.

Pray daily. Talk to God. He is your Father now, and he delights to hear from his children.

Follow Jesus. Discipleship is a lifelong journey. Take it one day at a time, one step at a time, trusting him to lead you.

THE LAST WORD

"For God so loved the world, that He gave His only begotten Son, that whoever believes in Him shall not perish, but have eternal life."

God loved. God gave. You believed. You shall not perish. You have eternal life.

This is the gospel. This is the good news. This is the message that has changed the world and can change you.

Welcome to the family of God.

> *"The Spirit and the bride say, 'Come.' And let the one who hears say, 'Come.' And let the one who is thirsty come; let the one who wishes take the water of life without cost."* (Rev 22:17)

Come.

QUESTIONS FOR REFLECTION

- Why is "today" so important when it comes to believing in Christ?
- What does it mean to truly believe in Jesus—not just intellectually, but with your whole heart?

- If you have believed, what assurances does Scripture give you about your salvation?
- What practical steps will you take to grow in your new faith?
- Who can you tell about your decision to follow Christ?

A FINAL PRAYER

Father, I thank You for the gift of Your Son. I thank You for the gift of eternal life. I thank You that whoever believes in Him shall not perish. I have believed. I have received. I am Yours. Now help me to live as Your child. Help me to grow in grace and in the knowledge of my Lord Jesus Christ. Use me to tell others what You have done for me. And when my life on earth is over, bring me safely home to be with You forever. Until that day, keep me faithful. I ask this in Jesus' name. Amen.

EPILOGUE

A Final Word of Hope

"For God so loved the world, that He gave His only begotten Son, that whoever believes in Him shall not perish, but have eternal life."

—John 3:16 (NASB)

We have come to the end of our journey through the most famous verse in the Bible. We began with God—the eternal, all-powerful, all-knowing, everywhere-present, holy, and just God who initiates salvation. We examined His love—not sentimental affection, but self-giving, sacrificial, unconditional *agapē*. We marveled at the scope of that love—extending to the whole world, including you.

We then turned to the gift—the costliest gift ever given. God did not send an angel or a prophet; He gave His only begotten Son. We explored who this Son is—truly God and truly man, the unique one, the eternal Word made flesh. We stood at the cross and witnessed where love and justice meet, where the penalty for our sins was paid in full.

We considered the response God requires—faith that is more than intellectual assent, trust that is personal reliance on Christ alone. We examined repentance—the turn that changes everything, the about-face from sin to Savior. We faced the sobering reality of perishing—the judgment that awaits all who reject God's offer—and we glimpsed the glory of eternal life, both now and forever.

And finally, we addressed the objections that keep people from believing, and we extended the invitation: Will you come?

Now, as we part ways—you with this book, and I with my prayer for you—I want to leave you with a final word of hope.

HOPE FOR THE SEEKER

If you are still seeking—still weighing the evidence, still wrestling with questions, still unsure—take heart. God promises that those who seek Him will find Him. "You will seek Me and find Me when you search for Me with all your heart" (Jer 29:13). The fact that you have read this far suggests that something is stirring within you. That stirring may well be God Himself, drawing you to His Son.

Do not give up the search. Keep reading. Keep asking. Keep knocking. The door will open. Jesus Himself promised: "Ask, and it will be given to you; seek, and you will find; knock, and it will be opened to you" (Matthew 7:7).

HOPE FOR THE HESITANT

If you believe the message is true but are hesitating to respond—perhaps because of fear, or shame, or uncertainty about what others will think—hear this: There is no condemnation for those who are in Christ Jesus (Rom 8:1). Whatever you fear, it is nothing compared to the joy of knowing Christ. Whatever you might lose, it is nothing compared to what you will gain.

The prodigal son hesitated in the far country, wondering if his father would receive him. But when he finally came home, his father ran to meet him, embraced him, and threw a feast in his honor (Luke 15:20–24). Your heavenly Father is waiting with open arms. Do not let fear keep you in the far country.

HOPE FOR THE NEW BELIEVER

If you have trusted Christ while reading this book—if you have crossed the line from death to life—welcome to the family of God. You are now a child of the King, an heir of the promise, a citizen of heaven. The journey of a thousand miles has begun with a single step, and that step is the most important one you will ever take.

The road ahead will not always be easy. You will face temptations, trials, and doubts. But you do not walk alone. The Holy Spirit dwells within you. Christ intercedes for you. The Father watches over you. And a community of believers—the church—is ready to walk with you.

"He who began a good work in you will perfect it until the day of Christ Jesus" (Phil 1:6). God finishes what He starts. He will not abandon you. He will complete His work in you.

HOPE FOR THE WORLD

John 3:16 tells us that God loved the world. His love is not limited to a select few, a chosen nation, or a religious elite. His love extends to every tribe, tongue, people, and nation. Wherever you are reading this—in America or Africa, Europe or Asia, the Middle East or the Pacific Islands—the message is for you. The invitation is for you. The promise is for you.

And the same message that has reached you is meant to reach others through you. If you have believed, you are now an ambassador for Christ (2 Cor 5:20). The love you have received is meant to overflow to others. The hope you have found is meant to be shared. The gospel that saved you is the power of God for salvation to everyone who believes (Rom 1:16).

A FINAL PRAYER

I close this book as I began it—with prayer for you, the reader.

Father in heaven, I thank You for the one holding this book. You know their name, their story, their struggles, and their hopes. You know whether they have believed or are still seeking. You know the barriers that remain and the fears that linger.

I pray that the message of John 3:16 would take root in their heart. May they know—truly know—that You love them, that Christ died for them, and that eternal life is offered to them. Remove every obstacle. Overcome every objection. Draw them to Yourself with cords of lovingkindness.

And if they have believed, strengthen them. Establish them. Root them deeply in Your Word and Your church. Use them to spread the fragrance of Christ wherever they go. May their lives be a living testimony to the truth of John 3:16—that You so loved the world that You gave Your only Son.

In the name of Jesus Christ, who loved us and gave Himself for us, Amen.

The invitation of John 3:16 remains open. The door is not yet closed. Today, if you hear His voice, do not harden your heart (Heb 3:15). Come to Christ. Believe in Him. Receive the eternal life He offers.

And may the God of hope fill you with all joy and peace in believing, so that you will abound in hope by the power of the Holy Spirit (Rom 15:13).

Soli Deo Gloria

To God alone be the glory.

APPENDIX A

How to Study the Bible

If you have placed your faith in Jesus Christ, one of the most important habits you can develop is regular Bible reading and study. The Bible is God's Word—His revelation of Himself, His will, and His ways. Through Scripture, God speaks to His people. As you read and study the Bible, you will grow in your knowledge of God, your understanding of His purposes, and your ability to live a life that pleases Him.

This appendix provides practical guidance for those who are new to Bible study. Whether you have never opened a Bible or have read it casually for years, these principles will help you engage God's Word more deeply and fruitfully.

CHOOSE A GOOD BIBLE TRANSLATION

The Bible was originally written in Hebrew (Old Testament) and Greek (New Testament). Since most of us do not read these languages, we depend on translations. Several excellent English translations are available:

New American Standard Bible (NASB): Highly accurate, word-for-word translation. Excellent for detailed study.

English Standard Version (ESV): Combines accuracy with readability. Widely used in churches today.

New International Version (NIV): Balances accuracy with natural English expression. Very accessible.

Christian Standard Bible (CSB): Recent translation balancing faithfulness and clarity.

New King James Version (NKJV): Updates the classic King James while retaining its dignified style.

For serious study, I recommend the NASB or ESV. For devotional reading, the NIV or CSB are excellent choices. Avoid paraphrases (like The Message) as your primary Bible; while they can be helpful for fresh perspective, they are interpretations rather than translations.

ESTABLISH A REGULAR READING PLAN

Consistency matters more than quantity. It is better to read a small portion daily than to read large portions sporadically. Here are some approaches for new believers:

Start with the Gospel of John. You have just studied John 3:16; now read the entire Gospel to see the context and learn more about Jesus.

Move to the other Gospels. After John, read Matthew, Mark, and Luke to see Jesus from different perspectives.

Read Acts. This book shows how the early church lived and spread the gospel after Jesus' ascension.

Study the New Testament letters. Romans, Ephesians, Philippians, and 1 John are particularly helpful for new believers.

Explore the Old Testament. Genesis, Exodus, Psalms, Proverbs, and Isaiah are good starting points.

APPENDIX A

THE INDUCTIVE BIBLE STUDY METHOD

Inductive Bible study involves three steps: Observation, Interpretation, and Application.

Step 1: Observation—What does the text say?

Read the passage carefully, multiple times if possible. Ask questions like:

- Who is speaking? Who is the audience?
- What is happening? What actions are described?
- When and where does this take place?
- Are there repeated words, phrases, or themes?
- Are there contrasts, comparisons, or cause-and-effect relationships?

Step 2: Interpretation—What does the text mean?

After observing what the text says, determine what it meant to the original audience. Consider:

- The historical and cultural context
- The literary context (what comes before and after)
- The meaning of key words in the original language
- How this passage fits with the rest of Scripture

Step 3: Application—How should this text change my life?

The goal of Bible study is not merely knowledge but transformation. Ask:

- Is there a command to obey?

- Is there a promise to claim?
- Is there a sin to confess or avoid?
- Is there an example to follow?
- Is there a truth about God to worship?

HELPFUL STUDY TOOLS

Study Bible: The ESV Study Bible, NIV Study Bible, or NASB MacArthur Study Bible provide helpful notes, maps, and articles.

Concordance: Helps you find every occurrence of a word in Scripture.

Bible Dictionary: Explains the meaning of biblical terms, places, and people.

Commentary: Provides verse-by-verse explanation from trusted scholars.

Bible App: Apps like YouVersion, Blue Letter Bible, and Logos provide free access to translations, study tools, and reading plans.

PRAY BEFORE, DURING, AND AFTER

Bible study is a spiritual activity, not merely an intellectual exercise. Before you open God's Word, ask the Holy Spirit to illuminate your mind and heart. Pray with the psalmist: "Open my eyes, that I may behold wonderful things from Your law" (Ps 119:18). As you read, pause to respond in prayer—thanking God, confessing sin, asking for help. After you finish, commit to obeying what you have learned.

APPENDIX B

Finding a Bible-Believing Church

The Christian life is not meant to be lived in isolation. When you trusted Christ, you were not only reconciled to God—you were also joined to His people. The New Testament knows nothing of solitary Christians. Believers are described as members of a body (1 Cor 12), stones in a temple (1 Pet 2:5), and sheep in a flock (John 10). We need each other.

But not every organization that calls itself a "church" is faithful to Scripture. How do you find a church that will help you grow in Christ? This appendix provides guidance for your search.

ESSENTIAL CHARACTERISTICS OF A HEALTHY CHURCH

Look for a church that demonstrates these marks:

1. *Biblical Authority*

A healthy church believes that the Bible is the inspired, inerrant, and authoritative Word of God. Scripture—not tradition, experience, or cultural trends—is the final authority for faith and practice. The preaching should be expository, explaining and applying the text of Scripture rather than using the Bible as a springboard for the pastor's opinions.

2. *Gospel Centrality*

The gospel—the good news of salvation through Jesus Christ—should be central to everything the church does. Beware of churches that emphasize self-help, social programs, or political activism to the exclusion of the gospel. A good church will clearly proclaim that we are sinners, that Christ died for our sins, and that salvation comes through faith in Him alone.

3. *Sound Doctrine*

A healthy church holds to the historic doctrines of the Christian faith:

- The Trinity: One God in three persons—Father, Son, and Holy Spirit
- The deity and humanity of Jesus Christ
- The virgin birth, atoning death, bodily resurrection, and future return of Christ
- Salvation by grace alone through faith alone in Christ alone
- The reality of heaven and hell

4. *Faithful Ordinances*

Jesus instituted two ordinances for the church: baptism and the Lord's Supper (Communion). A healthy church practices these as Jesus commanded—baptism for believers as a public confession of faith, and the Lord's Supper as a regular remembrance of Christ's death.

5. *Loving Community*

Jesus said, "By this all men will know that you are My disciples, if you have love for one another" (John 13:35). A healthy church is not just a Sunday gathering but a caring community where members know each other, bear each other's burdens, and encourage each other in the faith.

6. Evangelistic Zeal

A church that truly believes the gospel will be eager to share it. Look for a church that takes the Great Commission seriously, supporting missions and actively seeking to reach the lost in its community.

7. Godly Leadership

The New Testament provides qualifications for church leaders (1 Tim 3:1–13; Titus 1:5–9). Elders and pastors should be men of godly character, able to teach, and committed to shepherding the flock. Beware of churches dominated by a single personality without accountability.

QUESTIONS TO ASK WHEN VISITING A CHURCH

- What does this church believe about the Bible? Is it the inspired, inerrant Word of God?
- How does someone become a Christian according to this church? (The answer should be faith in Christ alone.)
- What is the preaching like? Is it faithful exposition of Scripture?
- How can I get connected and grow in community?
- What opportunities exist for spiritual growth (Bible studies, discipleship, small groups)?
- Does this church practice church discipline and membership?

RED FLAGS TO AVOID

- The Bible is not treated as the final authority
- The gospel of grace is replaced with self-help or works-righteousness
- Essential doctrines (Trinity, deity of Christ, resurrection) are denied or minimized
- Financial manipulation or pressure for giving
- A controlling, authoritarian leadership culture
- Lack of accountability for the pastor or leaders

A WORD OF ENCOURAGEMENT

No church is perfect—because no church is made up of perfect people. You will not find a church that does everything exactly as you would prefer. What matters is finding a church that is faithful to Scripture, centered on the gospel, and committed to loving God and loving people. When you find such a church, commit to it. Join it. Serve in it. Grow with it. The Christian life is a team sport, and you need your teammates.

APPENDIX C

Recommended Resources for New Believers

The Christian life is a journey of lifelong learning. The following resources are recommended to help you grow in your faith. This comprehensive list provides a solid foundation for new believers, organized into categories to help you know where to start and how to progress.

BOOKS FOR NEW BELIEVERS

Understanding the Faith

Basic Christianity—John Stott: A clear presentation of who Jesus is and what it means to follow Him.

Knowing God—J. I. Packer: A classic exploration of God's character and attributes.

Essential Truths of the Christian Faith—R. C. Sproul: 102 short chapters on key Christian doctrines.

The Reason for God—Timothy Keller: Answers to common objections to Christianity.

The Cross of Christ—John Stott: A deep look at the meaning and power of the cross.

Concise Theology—J. I. Packer: Accessible summaries of major Christian doctrines.

Christian Beliefs—Wayne Grudem: A simplified version of his Systematic Theology for beginners.

The Case for Christ—Lee Strobel: Investigative journalist examines the evidence for Jesus.

The Gospel for Real Life—Jerry Bridges: How the gospel applies to everyday life.

What Is the Gospel?—Greg Gilbert: A short, clear explanation of the gospel message.

Growing in Christ

The Pursuit of Holiness—Jerry Bridges: Practical guidance on living a holy life.

Spiritual Disciplines for the Christian Life—Donald S. Whitney: Covers prayer, Bible reading, fasting, and other practices.

The Mortification of Sin—John Owen (abridged editions available): A Puritan classic on fighting sin.

Mere Christianity—C. S. Lewis: A compelling defense and explanation of the Christian faith.

Celebration of Discipline—Richard Foster: Classic work on spiritual disciplines.

The Practice of Godliness—Jerry Bridges: Companion to The Pursuit of Holiness, focusing on godly character.

Disciplines of a Godly Man—R. Kent Hughes: Practical guidance for men pursuing Christlikeness.

The Normal Christian Life—Watchman Nee: A devotional classic on living out the Christian life.

Holiness—J. C. Ryle: A timeless call to holy living.

Living the Cross-Centered Life—C. J. Mahaney: Keeping the gospel central in daily discipleship.

Understanding the Bible

God's Big Picture—Vaughan Roberts: Traces the storyline of the Bible from Genesis to Revelation.

How to Read the Bible for All Its Worth—Gordon D. Fee and Douglas Stuart: Practical guide to biblical interpretation.

The Drama of Scripture—Craig Bartholomew & Michael Goheen: The Bible as one grand narrative.

Living by the Book—Howard & William Hendricks: Step-by-step guide to personal Bible study.

Grasping God's Word—J. Scott Duvall & J. Daniel Hays: Hermeneutics for students and pastors.

The King in His Beauty—Thomas Schreiner: A biblical theology tracing God's kingdom through Scripture.

40 Questions About Interpreting the Bible—Robert Plummer: Accessible answers to common hermeneutical questions.

RECOMMENDED STUDY BIBLES

A study Bible provides not only the text of Scripture but also notes, introductions, maps, and theological insights to help you understand what you are reading.

ESV Study Bible—Comprehensive notes, theological articles, and maps; excellent for serious study.

NIV Study Bible—Clear explanations and accessible notes; widely used across denominations.

CSB Study Bible—Balanced scholarship with approachable language; strong for devotional use.

NLT Life Application Study Bible—Focuses on practical application of Scripture to daily life.

NKJV Study Bible—Trusted translation with detailed notes and cross-references.

The MacArthur Study Bible—Verse-by-verse notes; strong expository focus.

The Tony Evans Study Bible—Expository notes with practical application.

The Reformation Study Bible—Edited by R. C. Sproul; strong doctrinal and theological depth.

The Apologetics Study Bible—Addresses common objections and questions about the faith.

The Gospel Transformation Study Bible—Shows how every passage points to Christ and the gospel.

ONLINE RESOURCES

Desiring God (desiringgod.org)—Articles, sermons, and books by John Piper.

The Gospel Coalition (thegospelcoalition.org)—Articles, podcasts, and reviews from trusted evangelical voices.

Ligonier Ministries (ligonier.org)—Teaching from R. C. Sproul and other Reformed scholars.

Blue Letter Bible (blueletterbible.org)—Free Bible study tools, commentaries, and original language resources.

BibleProject (bibleproject.com)—Animated videos explaining biblical books and themes.

Grace to You (gty.org)—John MacArthur's verse-by-verse expository preaching.

Insight for Living (insight.org)—Dr. Chuck Swindoll's ministry.

In Touch Ministries (intouch.org)—Dr. Charles Stanley's teaching resources.

Tony Evans—The Urban Alternative (tonyevans.org)—Sermons and devotionals.

Truth For Life (truthforlife.org)—Alistair Begg's ministry.

PODCASTS AND SERMONS

Ask Pastor John—John Piper answers theological and practical questions.

Renewing Your Mind—R.C. Sproul's daily teaching broadcast.

Grace to You—John MacArthur's verse-by-verse Bible teaching.

The Briefing—Albert Mohler's daily analysis from a Christian worldview.

The Urban Alternative—Tony Evans' sermons and teaching ministry.

Truth For Life—Alistair Begg's expository preaching.

Love Worth Finding—Classic expository sermons from Adrian Rogers.

MOBILE APPS

YouVersion Bible App—Free access to hundreds of translations and reading plans.

ESV Bible App—Clean, simple interface for reading the ESV with study notes.

Dwell—Premium audio Bible with beautiful narration.

Logos Bible App—Advanced study tools and commentaries.

Blue Letter Bible App—Excellent for original language study.

Our Daily Bread App—Trusted daily devotionals.

RECOMMENDED READING PLAN FOR NEW BELIEVERS

The resources above may seem overwhelming. Here is a suggested pathway to help you know where to start and how to progress.

Stage 1: Start Here (First 3 Months)

Basic Christianity by John Stott

What Is the Gospel? by Greg Gilbert

NIV Study Bible or NLT Life Application Study Bible for daily reading

YouVersion Bible App with a 30-day Gospel of John reading plan

Find a Bible-believing church (see Appendix B)

Stage 2: Build Your Foundation (Months 4–6)

Knowing God by J. I. Packer

The Pursuit of Holiness by Jerry Bridges

God's Big Picture by Vaughan Roberts

Consider upgrading to ESV Study Bible or MacArthur Study Bible

Begin listening to Ask Pastor John or Truth For Life

Stage 3: Go Deeper (Months 7–12)

Mere Christianity by C. S. Lewis

Spiritual Disciplines for the Christian Life by Donald Whitney

How to Read the Bible for All Its Worth by Fee and Stuart

Explore the Reformation Study Bible or Gospel Transformation Study Bible

Download Logos or Blue Letter Bible for deeper study

Stage 4: Continue Growing (Year 2 and Beyond)

Essential Truths of the Christian Faith by R.C. Sproul

The Cross of Christ by John Stott

Holiness by J. C. Ryle

Consider the Apologetics Study Bible for defending your faith

Explore Grace to You, Ligonier, and The Gospel Coalition for ongoing growth

Remember: The goal is not to read everything but to grow steadily in your knowledge of God, your love for Christ, and your obedience to His Word. Take your time, and let the Holy Spirit guide your journey.

About the Author

Dr. Elijah Wreh is a pastor, theologian, and Bible teacher with over two decades of ministry experience. He holds a Doctor of Ministry degree and is currently a PhD candidate in Bible Exposition at Liberty University, with an expected completion date of 2028.

Born and raised in Liberia, West Africa, Dr. Wreh experienced firsthand the devastation of civil war and the hope that only the Gospel can bring. His journey from war-torn Liberia to pastoral ministry in the United States has given him a unique perspective on the universal need for salvation and the universal offer of grace in John 3:16.

Dr. Wreh is the founding pastor of The Anointed Church of Jesus Christ, where his ministry centers on discipleship training and expository preaching. His passion is to make the deep truths of Scripture accessible to ordinary people—to bridge the gap between the academy and the pew. He believes that sound theology should not remain in ivory towers but should transform lives in living rooms, hospital rooms, and prison cells.

As a scholar, Dr. Elijah Wreh specializes in Bible Exposition with particular emphasis on Old and New Testament interpretation, Hebrew exegesis, and the theological unity of Scripture. His academic work integrates rigorous textual analysis with pastoral application, reflecting his commitment to the authority and inerrancy of Scripture. Dr. Wreh stands firmly within the historic evangelical tradition and brings together scholarly precision and practical ministry experience in his preaching, teaching, and writing.

PUBLICATIONS

Medical Device Regulation: FDA-CDRH Manufacturing, Policies and Regulation Handbook (Elsevier, 2023)
The Beatitudes: An Exegetical and Theological Commentary (forthcoming)

His previously published work, *Medical Device Regulation* (Elsevier, 2023), demonstrates his capacity for comprehensive scholarly writing across disciplines.

Dr. Wreh wrote this book with one prayer: that God would use these words to bring many sons and daughters to glory.

Dr. Wreh currently resides in LaGrange, Ohio, with his wife, Gradieh, and their three children. When not studying, writing, or preaching, he enjoys reading church history, mentoring young pastors, and engaging in gospel conversations over shared meals.

For speaking inquiries, pastoral resources, or to share how this book has impacted you, please contact the author through the publisher.

Soli Deo Gloria

To God Alone Be the Glory

Bibliography

Beasley-Murray, George R. *Baptism in the New Testament*. Grand Rapids: Eerdmans, 1962.

Bonhoeffer, Dietrich. *The Cost of Discipleship*. Translated by R. H. Fuller. New York: Touchstone, 1995.

Carson, D. A. *The Gospel According to John*. The Pillar New Testament Commentary. Grand Rapids: Eerdmans, 1991.

———. *How Long, O Lord? Reflections on Suffering and Evil*. 2nd ed. Grand Rapids: Baker Academic, 2006.

Cicero, Marcus Tullius. *The Verrine Orations*. Translated by L. H. G. Greenwood. 2 vols. Loeb Classical Library. Cambridge: Harvard University Press, 1928–1935.

Lewis, C. S. *The Four Loves*. New York: Harcourt, 1960.

———. *The Great Divorce*. New York: HarperOne, 2001.

———. *Mere Christianity*. New York: HarperOne, 2001.

———. *The Problem of Pain*. New York: HarperOne, 2001.

New American Standard Bible. La Habra, CA: The Lockman Foundation, 1995.

Pascal, Blaise. *Pensées*. Translated by A. J. Krailsheimer. London: Penguin, 1966.

Plantinga, Alvin. *God, Freedom, and Evil*. Grand Rapids: Eerdmans, 1977.

Stott, John R. W. *The Cross of Christ*. Downers Grove: InterVarsity Press, 1986.

Index

assurance of salvation, 83, 165
atonement, 98

belief, 7–15, 22, 25, 27, 28, 30–33, 35, 36, 46, 49, 52, 53, 60–63, 80–85, 87, 88, 90, 91, 94, 96, 98–101, 104, 108, 112, 114, 115, 120, 126–29, 131–33, 140, 154, 155, 157, 160–65, 167–70, 172, 175–77, 179, 180, 184, 187
Bonhoeffer, Dietrich, 150, 189
born again, 9, 107

Calvin, John, 71, 189
Carson, D. A., 52, 189
church, 31, 58, 65, 112, 156, 164, 169–72, 175–78, 184, 187, 188
common objections to faith, 14, 65, 73, 82, 85, 90, 99, 123, 155–57, 167, 169, 170, 182
condemnation, 45–47, 106, 126, 127, 129, 168
counting the cost, 13, 149, 151
covenant, 30, 31, 53
cross, the, 6, 7, 13, 15, 20, 43, 44, 56, 65–75, 90, 92, 95, 96, 100, 113, 115, 127, 148, 151, 152, 160, 162, 167, 168, 179–82, 185, 188, 189

death, 17, 20, 24, 43–46, 56, 57, 59, 60, 62, 65, 66, 70, 71, 73, 74, 84, 86, 91, 92, 95–99, 101, 105, 113, 121–23, 126, 128, 132–35, 140–43, 150, 160–62, 168, 176, 188
discipleship, 9, 13, 27, 30, 61, 71, 82, 90, 100, 148–52, 156, 161, 164, 165, 174, 176, 177, 179, 180, 187, 189
doubt, 65, 73, 82, 85, 90, 99, 155, 169

Ephesians 2, 17, 31, 45, 82, 86, 133, 139
eternal life, 7, 8, 10 14, 22, 42, 43, 45, 46, 61, 84, 86, 87, 90, 91, 99, 120, 121, 131, 132, 135, 136, 142, 149, 154, 160, 162–65, 167, 170
eternal punishment, 121, 122
evangelism, 30, 31, 40, 41, 123, 167, 177, 182, 187

faith, 7–9, 11, 13, 19, 25, 45, 46, 52, 53, 56, 68, 71, 74, 80–87, 90, 91, 93, 96–102, 104, 112, 114, 129, 132, 138, 142, 143, 155, 156, 161–63, 165, 167, 171, 172, 175–80, 182, 185
"For God" (John 3:16), 3–7, 164, 167

forgiveness, 20, 48, 56, 59, 61, 69–71, 82, 93, 107, 112, 114, 115, 157, 162
free will, 69, 107, 189

Genesis 3, 41, 45, 54, 67, 105
God, attributes of, 22, 29–31, 43, 47, 58, 68, 70, 73, 74, 90, 95, 98, 100, 107, 123, 124, 126, 129, 133, 167, 169, 170, 174, 176, 180, 185
God, initiates salvation, 3–7, 164, 167
God, love of, 3–7, 16, 17, 19–22, 32, 52, 133, 164, 167
gospel, 8–10, 14, 20, 31–33, 45, 46, 52, 53, 65–67, 80, 81, 86, 87, 91, 94, 96, 107, 112, 114, 120, 124, 126–28, 154, 157, 159, 164, 169, 172, 176–78, 180, 182, 184, 185, 187–89
grace, 5, 10, 13, 18, 29, 33, 44–46, 48–50, 69, 82, 83, 86, 92, 96, 97, 109, 113, 123, 124, 135, 162, 165, 176, 178, 182, 183, 185, 187

"His Only Begotten Son" (John 3:16), 5–7, 11, 22, 51–63, 164, 167
heaven, 10, 17, 22, 27, 41–43, 45, 48, 53, 56, 58, 60, 61, 63, 69, 81, 92, 94, 95, 97, 98, 104, 105, 108, 109, 115, 122, 124, 133, 134, 136, 140, 142, 150, 155, 168, 169, 176
hell, 7, 10, 11, 14, 15, 33, 36, 42, 58, 69, 98, 99, 110, 112–14, 120–29, 133, 134, 149, 163–65, 167, 176
Holy Spirit, 30, 31, 43, 95, 107, 112, 133, 138, 170, 174, 176, 185
hope, 31, 47, 61, 83, 85, 98, 100, 101, 120, 125, 126, 132, 133, 136, 140, 142, 167–70, 187
humility, 44, 48, 56, 92, 134, 151

incarnation, 56, 62, 92
invitation, 13, 14, 23, 34, 35, 49, 61, 80, 81, 87, 100, 101, 151, 167, 169, 170
Isaiah 53, 44, 67

Jesus Christ, deity of, 6, 8, 42, 52–54, 60–62, 66, 74, 94, 95, 97, 100, 101, 132, 160, 162, 178
Jesus Christ, humanity of, 55, 62
Jesus Christ, identity of, 35, 54, 55, 95, 141, 155, 156
Jesus Christ, only begotten Son, 5–7, 11, 22, 52, 53, 58, 60–63, 92, 164, 167
Jesus Christ, sacrifice of, 16, 19, 20, 22, 24, 41, 43, 44, 46, 48, 58–60, 68, 69, 72, 74, 94, 96, 97, 99, 100, 124, 128, 129, 170
Jesus Christ, as Savior, 9, 27, 30, 32, 33, 55, 56, 58, 60, 63, 88, 93, 94, 100, 101, 107, 112, 136, 160–62, 167, 176
John 3:16, 6, 7, 9–11, 13–17, 19, 20, 22, 27–31, 34, 40, 41, 43, 55, 58, 61, 65, 86, 93, 126, 133, 139, 167, 169, 170, 172, 187
John 3:17, 23
John 3:18, 12, 40, 67
John 3:36, 87, 132, 163
judgment, 10, 17, 20–22, 28, 52, 57, 61, 67, 68, 74, 75, 87, 96, 106, 109–11, 113, 114, 120, 122–29, 132, 156, 159, 160, 162, 167

justification, 45, 47, 48, 68, 82, 83, 85, 86, 96, 106, 109, 132, 138

kingdom of God, 9, 81, 150, 155

Lewis, C. S., 61, 63, 124, 142, 180, 184, 189
love, 3–7, 10, 11, 15–25, 27–36, 40, 43, 44, 49, 50, 52, 62, 68–71, 73–75, 86, 95, 100, 105, 109, 113, 115, 120, 123–25, 133–36, 138, 139, 141, 150, 155, 156, 162, 164, 167, 169, 170, 176, 178, 183, 185, 189
Luther, Martin, 71, 189

mercy, 17, 46, 48, 50, 56, 71, 83, 97, 107, 109, 113, 115, 121, 133, 154

new believer, 168, 172, 179

obedience, 22, 43, 47, 85, 87, 111, 161, 173, 174

Pascal, Blaise, 189
perishing, 7, 10, 11, 14, 15, 33, 36, 42, 58, 69, 98, 99, 110, 112, 114, 120, 121, 123–29, 133, 134, 149, 163–65, 167
Plantinga, Alvin, 189
prayer, 24, 29, 36, 47, 48, 50, 63, 71, 75, 87, 98, 101, 109, 115, 129, 131, 136, 139, 142, 152, 157, 162, 164, 165, 168, 169, 174, 180, 188
prayer of salvation, 162, 165

redemption, 19, 32, 45, 56, 58, 67, 69, 73, 75, 96, 98, 127, 162
repentance, 9, 33, 36, 70, 87, 103–15, 121, 122, 125, 127, 161, 167
resurrection, 30, 54, 59, 93, 95–97, 99–101, 114, 131, 133–36, 160, 162, 176, 178
righteousness, 6, 18, 21, 22, 41, 46–48, 50, 59, 67, 68, 70, 75, 83, 85, 86, 96, 97, 107, 113, 114, 122–27, 129, 138, 139, 154, 161, 178
Romans 5:8, 17, 73
Romans 6:23, 45, 126, 135
Romans 8, 24, 42, 127, 168

sacrifice, 16, 19, 20, 22, 24, 43, 58, 59, 68, 72, 94, 96, 97, 124, 128, 129, 167
salvation, 7, 8, 10, 13, 15, 17, 20, 29, 32, 33, 35, 44–49, 56–58, 60, 62, 65, 68, 70–72, 75, 80–86, 90, 91, 93, 94, 96–98, 101, 105, 107, 110, 120, 127–29, 138, 148, 154, 155, 159–63, 165, 167, 169, 176, 187
sanctification, 138, 142, 180
"Shall Not Perish" (John 3:16), 7, 10, 11, 15, 112, 119–29, 164, 167
sin, 3, 5–9, 17, 20–24, 27, 28, 33, 35, 41–48, 50, 54–63, 67–75, 82, 83, 86, 87, 90, 91, 93, 96–98, 100, 101, 104–9, 111–15, 120, 123–29, 132, 135, 139–42, 150, 154, 156, 159–62, 167, 169, 171, 174–77, 180
"So Loved" (John 3:16), 3–7, 14–25, 164, 167
Stott, John, 71, 179, 184, 185, 189
substitution, 57, 66, 71
suffering, 20, 44, 67, 100, 120, 131, 135, 152, 189

"That He Gave" (John 3:16), 4–7, 19, 39–50, 164, 167

"The World" (John 3:16), 3–7, 17, 19–22, 27–36, 164, 167
Trinity, 17, 41, 92, 176, 178
truth, 5, 11, 18, 22, 23, 30, 33, 40, 53, 55, 59, 60, 62, 63, 70, 74, 75, 81–83, 86, 92, 94, 98, 99, 105–8, 110–14, 120, 123, 127, 131, 132, 138, 155, 156, 162, 168, 170, 174, 179, 183–85, 187
urgency of belief, 15, 86, 127–29, 158–65

"Whoever Believes" (John 3:16), 7, 8, 10, 11, 13–15, 35, 79–88, 100, 112, 126, 128, 129, 164, 165, 167
world, scope of God's love, 3, 4, 15, 18, 27–36, 141, 167
wrath of God, 20–22, 57, 68, 75, 87, 111, 122, 126–29

www.ingramcontent.com/pod-product-compliance
Lightning Source LLC
LaVergne TN
LVHW050630100826
845148LV00011B/1808

* 9 7 9 8 3 8 5 2 7 6 6 1 5 *